BUSHIDO
ILLUSTRATED

TO MY BELOVED UNCLE
TOKITOSHI OTA
WHO TAUGHT ME TO REVERE THE PAST
AND TO ADMIRE THE DEEDS OF THE SAMURAI
I DEDICATE THIS LITTLE BOOK.

BUSHIDO ILLUSTRATED

THE SOUL OF JAPAN

INAZŌ NITOBE

amber
BOOKS

First published in 2021

Reprinted in 2023, 2025 twice

Amber Books Ltd
United House
North Road
London N7 9DP
United Kingdom
www.amberbooks.co.uk
Instagram: amberbooksltd
Facebook: amberbooks
Twitter: @amberbooks
Pinterest: amberbooksltd

ISBN: 978-1-83886-089-9

Project Editor: Michael Spilling
Design: Keren Harragan
Picture Research: Terry Forshaw

Printed and bound in China

PICTURE CREDITS:
Alamy: 12 (Artokoloro), 15 (CPA Media), 18 (Granger Historical Picture Archive), 22 (The Picture Art Collection), 25 (Granger Historical Picture Archive), 29 (Artokoloro), 35 & 36 (Art Collection 2), 39 (Japan Art Collection), 51 (CPA Media), 59 (World History Archive), 69 (CPA Media), 74 (Artokoloro), 82 (Buyenlarge/UIG), 84 (Historica Graphica/Heritage Images), 87 (CPA Media), 90 (Prisma by Dukas), 98 (World History Archive), 107 (Jonathan O'Rourke), 117 (Florilegius), 118 (Japan Art Collection), 126 (WBC ART), 141 (Everett Collection), 143 (Album/British Library), 145 (Chronicle of World History), 151 (agefotostock)
Bridgeman Images: 17 (Freer Gallery of Art, Smithsonian Institution/Gift of Charles Lang Freer), 81 (Pictures from History/Woodbury & Page)
Getty Images: 77 (Sepia Times), 89 (De Agostini), 111 (Sepia Times), 121 (John Stevenson/Corbis), 148 (Werner Forman)
Library of Congress: front cover, 53, 64, 67, 95, 104, 133, 154
Metropolitan Museum of Art, New York: 9, 43–48 all, 57, 63, 71, 112, 114, 122, 125, 129, 134, 158
Minneapolis Institute of Art: 72
Philadelphia Museum of Art: 11 (Gift of Mrs John D Rockefeller, Jr, 1946, 1946-51-8), 153 (Gift of Ann E and Donald W McPhail, 2012, 2012-25-54), 157 (Purchased with funds contributed by the E Rhodes and Leona B Carpenter Foundation, 1989, 1989-47-470157)
Shutterstock: 101 (Marzolino)

TRADITIONAL CHINESE BOOKBINDING

This book has been produced using traditional Chinese bookbinding techniques, using a method that was developed during the Ming Dynasty (1368–1644) and remained in use until the adoption of Western binding techniques in the early 1900s. In traditional Chinese binding, single sheets of paper are printed on one side only, and each sheet is folded in half, with the printed pages on the outside. The book block is then sandwiched between two boards and sewn together through punched holes close to the cut edges of the folded sheets.

Contents

Preface to the first edition

About ten years ago, while spending a few days under the hospitable roof of the distinguished Belgian jurist, the late lamented M. de Laveleye, our conversation turned, during one of our rambles, to the subject of religion. "Do you mean to say," asked the venerable professor, "that you have no religious instruction in your schools?" On my replying in the negative he suddenly halted in astonishment, and in a voice which I shall not easily forget, he repeated: "No religion! How do you impart moral education?" The question stunned me at the time. I could give no ready answer, for the moral precepts I learned in my childhood days were not given in schools; and not until I began to analyze the different elements that formed my notions of right and wrong, did I find that it was *Bushido*[1] that breathed them into my nostrils.

The direct inception of this little book is due to the frequent queries put by my wife as to the reasons why such and such ideas and customs prevail in Japan.

In my attempts to give satisfactory replies to M. de Laveleye and to my wife, I found that without understanding Feudalism and Bushido, the moral ideas of present Japan are a sealed volume.

Taking advantage of enforced idleness on account of long illness, I put down in the order now presented to the public some of the answers given in our household conversation. They consist mainly of what I was taught and told in my youthful days, when Feudalism was still in force.

Between Lafcadio Hearn and Mrs. Hugh Fraser on one side and Sir Ernest Satow and Professor Chamberlain on the other, it is indeed discouraging to write anything Japanese in English. The only advantage I have over them is that I can assume the attitude of a personal defendant, while these distinguished writers are at best solicitors and attorneys. I have often thought, "Had I their gift of language, I would present the cause of Japan in more eloquent terms!" But one who speaks in a borrowed tongue should be thankful if he can just make himself intelligible.

All through the discourse I have tried to illustrate whatever points I have made with parallel examples from European history and literature, believing that these will aid in bringing the subject nearer to the comprehension of foreign readers.

Should any of my allusions to religious subjects and to religious workers be thought slighting, I trust my attitude towards Christianity itself will not be questioned. It is with ecclesiastical methods and with the forms which obscure the teachings of Christ, and not with the teachings themselves, that I have little sympathy. I believe in the religion taught by Him and handed down to us in the New Testament, as well as in the law written in the heart. Further, I believe that God hath made a testament which may be called "old" with every people and nation—Gentile or Jew, Christian or Heathen. As to the rest of my theology, I need not impose upon the patience of the public.

INAZO NITOBE, Malvern, Pa., Twelfth Month, 1899

[1] Pronounced *Boó-shee-doh.* In putting Japanese words and names into English, Hepburn's rule is followed, that the vowels should be used as in European languages, and the consonants as in English.

Extract from the preface to the tenth and revised edition

In making emendations and additions for the present edition, I have largely confined them to concrete examples. I still continue to regret, as I indeed have never ceased to do, my inability to add a chapter on Filial Piety, which is considered one of the two wheels of the chariot of Japanese ethics—Loyalty being the other. My inability is due rather to my ignorance of the Western sentiment in regard to this particular virtue, than to ignorance of our own attitude towards it, and I cannot draw comparisons satisfying to my own mind. I hope one day to enlarge upon this and other topics at some length. All the subjects that are touched upon in these pages are capable of further amplification and discussion; but I do not now see my way clear to make this volume larger than it is.

INAZO NITOBE, Kyoto, 1905

Note on the Author

Born in 1862, Inazo Nitobe began learning English at the age of nine. He studied at Sapporo Agricultural College and entered Tokyo Imperial University in 1883, studying economics and English literature. He later traveled to the United States, where he studied politics and international relations at John Hopkins University from 1884 to 1887. In Germany from 1887, he studied at several universities, receiving a doctorate in agricultural economics. By the time he returned to Japan in 1891, he had published books both in English and German. Nitobe taught at Sapporo Agricultural College from 1891 to 1897, before taking a sabbatical. During this period he spent some time in California and Pennsylvania, where he wrote *Bushido: The Soul of Japan*, which was published in 1900.

From 1903 to 1919 he held a professorship at Kyoto Imperial University and was headmaster of the First Higher School in Tokyo. He also held public offices, serving as a colonial administrator in Taiwan from 1901 to 1903. Following the end of World War I, he attended the Versailles Peace Conference in 1918, then became an under secretary of the newly-formed League of Nations. He was also the chairman of the Institute of Pacific Relations from 1929 to 1933. In 1933, while leading a Japanese delegation to an international conference in Canada, he developed pneumonia and died in hospital in Victoria, British Columbia.

Nitobe was a prolific writer. He published many scholarly books as well as books for general readers. In the West, *Bushido: The Soul of Japan* has been a bestseller since the outbreak of the Russo-Japanese War of 1904–05, and has been translated into dozens of languages.

CHAPTER 1

武士道の倫理

Bushido as an Ethical System

Chivalry is a flower no less indigenous to the soil of Japan than its emblem, the cherry blossom; nor is it a dried-up specimen of an antique virtue preserved in the herbarium of our history. It is still a living object of power and beauty among us; and if it assumes no tangible shape or form, it none the less scents the moral atmosphere, and makes us aware that we are still under its potent spell. The conditions of society which brought it forth and nourished it have long disappeared; but as those far-off stars which once were and are not, still continue to shed their rays upon us, so the light of chivalry, which was a child of feudalism, still illuminates our moral path, surviving its mother institution. It is a pleasure to me to reflect upon this subject in the language of Burke, who uttered the well-known touching eulogy over the neglected bier of its European prototype.

It argues a sad defect of information concerning the Far East, when so erudite a scholar as Dr. George Miller did not hesitate to affirm that chivalry, or any other similar institution, has never existed either among the nations of antiquity or among the modern Orientals.[2] Such ignorance, however, is amply excusable, as the third edition of the good Doctor's work appeared the same year that Commodore Perry was knocking at the portals of our exclusivism. More than a decade later, about the time that our feudalism was in the last throes of existence, Karl Marx, writing his *Das Kapital*, called the attention of his readers to the peculiar advantage of studying the social and political institutions of feudalism, as then to be seen in living form only in Japan. I would likewise invite the Western

[2] *History Philosophically Illustrated* (3rd Ed. 1853), Vol. II, p. 2.

An early nineteenth century hanging scroll entitled 'A Courtesan and her Attendant under a Cherry Tree', by Utagawa Toyoharu (1735–1814).

historical and ethical student to the study of chivalry in the Japan of the present.

Enticing as is a historical disquisition on the comparison between European and Japanese feudalism and chivalry, it is not the purpose of this paper to enter into it at length. My attempt is rather to relate, *firstly,* the origin and sources of our chivalry; *secondly,* its character and teaching; *thirdly,* its influence among the masses; and, *fourthly,* the continuity and permanence of its influence. Of these several points, the first will be only brief and cursory, or else I should have to take my readers into the devious paths of our national history; the second will be dwelt upon at greater length, as being most likely to interest students of International Ethics and Comparative Ethology in our ways of thought and action; and the rest will be dealt with as corollaries.

The Japanese word which I have roughly rendered Chivalry, is, in the original, more expressive than Horsemanship. *Bu-shi-do* means literally "Military-Knight-Ways"—the ways which fighting nobles should observe in their daily life as well as in their vocation; in a word, the "Precepts of Knighthood," the *noblesse oblige* of the warrior class. Having thus given its literal significance, I may be allowed henceforth to use the word in the original. The use of the original term is also advisable for this reason, that a teaching so circumscribed and unique, engendering a cast of mind and character so peculiar, so local, must wear the badge of its singularity on its face; then, some words have a national timbre so expressive of race characteristics that the best of translators can do them but scant justice, not to say positive injustice and grievance. Who can improve by translation what the German "*Gemüth*" signifies, or who does not feel the difference between the two words verbally so closely allied as the English gentleman and the French *gentilhomme*?

Bushido, then, is the code of moral principles which the knights were required or instructed to observe. It is not a written code; at best it consists of a few maxims handed down from mouth to mouth or coming from the pen of some well-known warrior or savant. More frequently it is a code unuttered and unwritten, possessing all the more the powerful sanction of veritable deed, and of a law written on the fleshly tablets of the heart. It was founded not on the creation of one brain, however able, or on the life of a single personage, however renowned. It was an organic growth

A traditional mounted samurai is attended by his servant. The horses ridden by samurai were a native breed, Kisouma, which resembled stocky ponies.

The warrior Okura Ubain Yorifusa kneels at the feet of Minamoto no Yoritomo (1147–1199), a colour woodcut by Yashima Gakutei (1820).

of decades and centuries of military career. It, perhaps, fills the same position in the history of ethics that the English Constitution does in political history; yet it has had nothing to compare with the Magna Carta or the Habeas Corpus Act. True, early in the seventeenth century Military Statutes (*Buké Hatto*) were promulgated; but their thirteen short articles were taken up mostly with marriages, castles, leagues, etc., and didactic regulations were but meagerly touched upon. We cannot, therefore, point out any definite time and place and say, "Here is its fountain head." Only as it attains consciousness in the feudal age, its origin, in respect to time, may be identified with feudalism. But feudalism itself is woven of many threads, and Bushido shares its intricate nature. As in England the political institutions of feudalism may be said to date from the Norman Conquest, so we may say that in Japan its rise was simultaneous with the ascendency of Yoritomo, late in the twelfth century. As, however, in England, we find the social elements of feudalism far back in the period previous to William the Conqueror, so, too, the germs of feudalism in Japan had been long existent before the period I have mentioned.

Again, in Japan as in Europe, when feudalism was formally inaugurated, the professional class of warriors naturally came into prominence. These were known as *samurai*, meaning literally, like the old English *cniht* (knecht, knight), guards or attendants—resembling in character the *soldurii* whom Caesar mentioned as existing in Aquitania, or the *comitati*, who, according to Tacitus, followed Germanic chiefs in his time; or, to take a still later parallel, the *milites medii* that one reads about in the history of Mediaeval Europe. A Sinico-Japanese word *Bu-ké* or *Bu-shi* (Fighting Knights) was also adopted in common use. They were a privileged class, and must originally have been a rough breed who made fighting their vocation. This class was naturally recruited, in a long period of constant warfare, from the manliest and the most adventurous, and all the while the process of elimination went on, the timid and the feeble being sorted out, and only "a rude race, all masculine, with brutish strength," to borrow Emerson's phrase, surviving to form families and the ranks of the *samurai*. Coming to profess great honor and great privileges, and correspondingly great responsibilities, they soon felt the need of a common standard of behavior, especially as they were always on a belligerent footing and belonged to different clans. Just as physicians limit competition among themselves by professional courtesy, just as lawyers sit in courts of honor

in cases of violated etiquette, so must also warriors possess some resort for final judgment on their misdemeanors.

Fair play in fight! What fertile germs of morality lie in this primitive sense of savagery and childhood. Is it not the root of all military and civic virtues? We smile (as if we had outgrown it!) at the boyish desire of the small Britisher, Tom Brown, "to leave behind him the name of a fellow who never bullied a little boy or turned his back on a big one." And yet, who does not know that this desire is the corner-stone on which moral structures of mighty dimensions can be reared? May I not go even so far as to say that the gentlest and most peace-loving of religions endorses this aspiration? This desire of Tom's is the basis on which the greatness of England is largely built, and it will not take us long to discover that Bushido does not stand on a lesser pedestal. If fighting in itself, be it offensive or defensive, is, as Quakers rightly testify, brutal and wrong, we can still say with Lessing, "We know from what failings our virtue springs."[3] "Sneaks" and "cowards" are epithets of the worst opprobrium to healthy, simple natures. Childhood begins life with these notions, and knighthood also; but, as life grows larger and its relations many-sided, the early faith seeks sanction from higher authority and more rational sources for its own justification, satisfaction and development. If military interests had operated alone, without higher moral support, how far short of chivalry would the ideal of knighthood have fallen! In Europe, Christianity, interpreted with concessions convenient to chivalry, infused it nevertheless with spiritual data. "Religion, war and glory were the three souls of a perfect Christian knight," says Lamartine. In Japan there were several sources of Bushido.

[3] Ruskin was one of the most gentle-hearted and peace-loving men that ever lived. Yet he believed in war with all the fervor of a worshiper of the strenuous life. "When I tell you," he says in the *Crown of Wild Olive*, "that war is the foundation of all the arts, I mean also that it is the foundation of all the high virtues and faculties of men. It is very strange to me to discover this, and very dreadful, but I saw it to be quite an undeniable fact. ... I found in brief, that all great nations learned their truth of word and strength of thought in war; that they were nourished in war and wasted by peace, taught by war and deceived by peace; trained by war and betrayed by peace; in a word, that they were born in war and expired in peace."

A bushi *(warrior) sits with his* katana *sword. By the end of the twelfth century, the term 'samurai' had become synonymous with* bushi.

CHAPTER 2

武士道の始まり

Sources of Bushido

I may begin with Buddhism. It furnished a sense of calm trust in Fate, a quiet submission to the inevitable, that stoic composure in sight of danger or calamity, that disdain of life and friendliness with death. A foremost teacher of swordsmanship, when he saw his pupil master the utmost of his art, told him, "Beyond this my instruction must give way to Zen teaching." "Zen" is the Japanese equivalent for the Dhyâna, which "represents human effort to reach through meditation zones of thought beyond the range of verbal expression."[4] Its method is contemplation, and its purport, as far as I understand it, to be convinced of a principle that underlies all phenomena, and, if it can, of the Absolute itself, and thus to put oneself in harmony with this Absolute. Thus defined, the teaching was more than the dogma of a sect, and whoever attains to the perception of the Absolute raises himself above mundane things and awakes, "to a new Heaven and a new Earth."

What Buddhism failed to give, Shintoism offered in abundance. Such loyalty to the sovereign, such reverence for ancestral memory, and such filial piety as are not taught by any other creed, were inculcated by the Shinto doctrines, imparting passivity to the otherwise arrogant character of the samurai. Shinto theology has no place for the dogma of "original sin." On the contrary, it believes in the innate goodness and God-like purity of the human soul, adoring it as the adytum from which divine oracles are proclaimed. Everybody has observed that the Shinto shrines are conspicuously devoid of objects and instruments of worship, and that a plain mirror hung in the sanctuary forms the

[4] Lafcadio Hearn, "Exotics and Retrospectives", p. 84.

A Shinto priest offers blessings to a Japanese family.

Ise Grand Shrine, the most sacred Shintō shrine in Japan, as depicted in a late sixteenth century painting attributed to Tosa Mitsunobu.

essential part of its furnishing. The presence of this article is easy to explain: it typifies the human heart, which, when perfectly placid and clear, reflects the very image of the Deity. When you stand, therefore, in front of the shrine to worship, you see your own image reflected on its shining surface, and the act of worship is tantamount to the old Delphic injunction, "Know Thyself." But self-knowledge does not imply, either in the Greek or Japanese teaching, knowledge of the physical part of man, not his anatomy or his psycho-physics; knowledge was to be of a moral kind, the introspection of our moral nature. Mommsen, comparing the Greek and the Roman, says that when the former worshiped he raised his eyes to heaven, for his prayer was contemplation, while the latter veiled his head, for his was reflection. Essentially like the Roman conception of religion, our reflection brought into prominence not so much the moral as the national consciousness of the individual. Its nature-worship endeared the country to our inmost souls, while its ancestor-worship, tracing from lineage to lineage, made the Imperial family the fountain-head of the whole nation. To us the country is more than land and soil from which to mine gold or to reap grain—it is the sacred abode of the gods, the spirits of our forefathers: to us the Emperor is more than the Arch Constable of a *Rechtsstaat,* or even the Patron of a *Culturstaat*—he is the bodily representative of Heaven on earth, blending in his person its power and its mercy. If what M. Boutmy[5] says is true of English royalty—that it "is not only the image of authority, but the author and symbol of national unity," as I believe it to be, doubly and trebly may this be affirmed of royalty in Japan.

The tenets of Shintoism cover the two predominating features of the emotional life of our race—Patriotism and Loyalty. Arthur May Knapp very truly says: "In Hebrew literature it is often difficult to tell whether the writer is speaking of God or of the Commonwealth; of heaven or of Jerusalem; of the Messiah or of the nation itself."[6] A similar confusion may be noticed in the nomenclature of our national faith. I said confusion, because it will be so deemed by a logical intellect on account of its verbal ambiguity; still, being a framework of national instinct and race feelings, Shintoism never pretends to a systematic philosophy or a rational theology. This religion—or, is it not more correct to say, the race emotions which this religion expressed—thoroughly imbued

5 *The English People,* p. 188.

6 *Feudal and Modern Japan* Vol. I, p. 183.

Bushido with loyalty to the sovereign and love of country. These acted more as impulses than as doctrines; for Shintoism, unlike the Mediaeval Christian Church, prescribed to its votaries scarcely any *credenda*, furnishing them at the same time with an *agenda* of a straightforward and simple type.

As to strictly ethical doctrines, the teachings of Confucius were the most prolific source of Bushido. His enunciation of the five moral relations between master and servant (the governing and the governed), father and son, husband and wife, older and younger brother, and between friend and friend, was but a confirmation of what the race instinct had recognized before his writings were introduced from China. The calm, benignant, and worldly-wise character of his politico-ethical precepts was particularly well suited to the samurai, who formed the ruling class. His aristocratic and conservative tone was well adapted to the requirements of these warrior statesmen. Next to Confucius, Mencius exercised an immense authority over Bushido. His forcible and often quite democratic theories were exceedingly taking to sympathetic natures, and they were even thought dangerous to, and subversive of, the existing social order, hence his works were for a long time under censure. Still, the words of this master mind found permanent lodgment in the heart of the samurai.

The writings of Confucius and Mencius formed the principal text-books for youths and the highest authority in discussion among the old. A mere acquaintance with the classics of these two sages was held, however, in no high esteem. A common proverb ridicules one who has only an intellectual knowledge of Confucius, as a man ever studious but ignorant of *Analects*. A typical samurai calls a literary savant a book-smelling sot. Another compares learning to an ill-smelling vegetable that must be boiled and boiled before it is fit for use. A man who has read a little smells a little pedantic, and a man who has read much smells yet more so; both are alike unpleasant. The writer meant thereby that knowledge becomes really such only when it is assimilated in the mind of the learner and shows in his character. An intellectual specialist was considered a machine. Intellect itself was considered subordinate to ethical emotion. Man and the universe were conceived to be alike spiritual and ethical. Bushido could not accept the judgment of Huxley, that the cosmic process was unmoral.

Bushido made light of knowledge as such. It was not pursued as an end in itself, but as a means to the attainment of wisdom. Hence, he who stopped short of this end was regarded no higher than a convenient machine, which could turn out poems and maxims at bidding. Thus, knowledge was conceived as identical with its practical application in life; and this Socratic doctrine found its greatest exponent in the Chinese philosopher, Wan Yang Ming, who never wearies of repeating, "To know and to act are one and the same."

I beg leave for a moment's digression while I am on this subject, inasmuch as some of the noblest types of *bushi* were strongly influenced by the teachings of this sage. Western readers will easily recognize in his writings many parallels to the New Testament. Making allowance for the terms peculiar to either teaching, the passage, "Seek ye first the kingdom of God and his righteousness; and all these things shall be added unto you," conveys a thought that may be found on almost any page of Wan Yang Ming. A Japanese disciple[7] of his says—"The lord of heaven and earth, of all living beings, dwelling in the heart of man, becomes his mind (*Kokoro*); hence a mind is a living thing, and is ever luminous;" and again, "The spiritual light of our essential being is pure, and is not affected by the will of man. Spontaneously springing up in our mind, it shows what is right and wrong: it is then called conscience; it is even the light that proceedeth from the god of heaven." How very much do these words sound like some passages from Isaac Pennington or other philosophic mystics! I am inclined to think that the Japanese mind, as expressed in the simple tenets of the Shinto religion, was particularly open to the reception of Yang Ming's precepts. He carried his doctrine of the infallibility of conscience to extreme transcendentalism, attributing to it the faculty to perceive, not only the distinction between right and wrong, but also the nature of psychical facts and physical phenomena. He went as far as, if not farther than, Berkeley and Fichte, in Idealism, denying the existence of things outside of human ken. If his system had all the logical errors charged to Solipsism, it had all the efficacy of strong conviction and its moral import in developing individuality of character and equanimity of temper cannot be gainsaid.

Thus, whatever the sources, the essential principles which Bushido imbibed from them and assimilated to itself, were few and simple. Few

[7] *Miwa Shissai.*

Yukimori (1543–76), a samurai from the Sengoku, or 'Warring States', period (1467–1615). He wears a suit of armor called tosei gusoku *('modern equipment') that was designed in the sixteenth century. Like many samurai, Yukimori never went into battle without the crescent moon ornament he wore on his helmet as a token of good luck.*

and simple as these were, they were sufficient to furnish a safe conduct of life even through the unsafest days of the most unsettled period of our nation's history. The wholesome, unsophisticated nature of our warrior ancestors derived ample food for their spirit from a sheaf of commonplace and fragmentary teachings, gleaned as it were on the highways and byways of ancient thought, and, stimulated by the demands of the age, formed from these gleanings a new and unique type of manhood. An acute French *savant*, M. de la Mazelière, thus sums up his impressions of the sixteenth century: "Toward the middle of the sixteenth century, all is confusion in Japan, in the government, in society, in the church. But the civil wars, the manners returning to barbarism, the necessity for each to execute justice for himself—these formed men comparable to those Italians of the sixteenth century, in whom Taine praises 'the vigorous initiative, the habit of sudden resolutions and desperate undertakings, the grand capacity to do and to suffer.' In Japan as in Italy 'the rude manners of the Middle Ages made of man a superb animal, wholly militant and wholly resistant.' And this is why the sixteenth century displays in the highest degree the principal quality of the Japanese race, that great diversity which one finds there between minds (*esprits*) as well as between temperaments. While in India and even in China men seem to differ chiefly in degree of energy or intelligence, in Japan they differ by originality of character as well. Now, individuality is the sign of superior races and of civilizations already developed. If we make use of an expression dear to Nietzsche, we might say that in Asia, to speak of humanity is to speak of its plains; in Japan as in Europe, one represents it above all by its mountains."

To the pervading characteristics of the men of whom M. de la Mazelière writes, let us now address ourselves. I shall begin with rectitude, or justice.

CHAPTER 3

正義

Rectitude or Justice

This is the most cogent precept in the code of the samurai. Nothing is more loathsome to him than underhand dealings and crooked undertakings. The conception of Rectitude may be erroneous—it may be narrow. A well-known *bushi* defines it as a power of resolution—"Rectitude is the power of deciding upon a certain course of conduct in accordance with reason, without wavering; to die when it is right to die, to strike when to strike is right." Another speaks of it in the following terms: "Rectitude is the bone that gives firmness and stature. As without bones the head cannot rest on the top of the spine, nor hands move nor feet stand, so without rectitude neither talent nor learning can make of a human frame a samurai. With it the lack of accomplishments is as nothing." Mencius calls Benevolence man's mind, and Rectitude or Righteousness his path. "How lamentable," he exclaims, "is it to neglect the path and not pursue it, to lose the mind and not know to seek it again! When men's fowls and dogs are lost, they know to seek for them again, but they lose their mind and do not know to seek for it." Have we not here "as in a glass darkly" a parable propounded three hundred years later in another clime and by a greater Teacher, who called Himself *the Way* of Righteousness, through whom the lost could be found? But I stray from my point. Righteousness, according to Mencius, is a straight and narrow path which a man ought to take to regain the lost paradise.

Even in the latter days of feudalism, when the long continuance of peace brought leisure into the life of the warrior class, and with it dissipations of all kinds and gentle accomplishments, the epithet *Gishi*

Mencius, also known as Mengzi (372–289 BCE), has often been described as the 'Second Sage' after Confucius.

(a man of rectitude) was considered superior to any name that signified mastery of learning or art. The Forty-seven Faithfuls—of whom so much is made in our popular education—are known in common parlance as the Forty-seven *Gishi.*

In times when cunning artifice was liable to pass for military tact and downright falsehood for *ruse de guerre,* this manly virtue, frank and honest, was a jewel that shone the brightest and was most highly praised. Rectitude is a twin brother to Valor, another martial virtue. But before proceeding to speak of Valor, let me linger a little while on what I may term a derivation from Rectitude, which, at first deviating slightly from its original, became more and more removed from it, until its meaning was perverted in the popular acceptance. I speak of *Gi-ri,* literally the Right Reason, but which came in time to mean a vague sense of duty which public opinion expected an incumbent to fulfil. In its original and unalloyed sense, it meant duty, pure and simple—hence, we speak of the *Giri* we owe to parents, to superiors, to inferiors, to society at large, and so forth. In these instances *Giri* is duty; for what else is duty than what Right Reason demands and commands us to do. Should not Right Reason be our categorical imperative?

Giri primarily meant no more than duty, and I dare say its etymology was derived from the fact that in our conduct, say to our parents, though love should be the only motive, lacking that, there must be some other authority to enforce filial piety; and they formulated this authority in *Giri.* Very rightly did they formulate this authority—*Giri*—since if love does not rush to deeds of virtue, recourse must be had to man's intellect and his reason must be quickened to convince him of the necessity of acting aright. The same is true of any other moral obligation. The instant Duty becomes onerous. Right Reason steps in to prevent our shirking it. *Giri* thus understood is a severe taskmaster, with a birch-rod in his hand to make sluggards perform their part. It is a secondary power in ethics; as a motive it is infinitely inferior to the Christian doctrine of love, which should be the law. I deem it a product of the conditions of an artificial society—of a society in which accident of birth and unmerited favour instituted class distinctions, in which the family was the social unit, in which seniority of age was of more account than superiority of talents, in which natural affections had often to succumb before arbitrary man-made customs. Because of this very artificiality, *Giri* in time degenerated into a vague sense of propriety called up to explain this and sanction that—as, for example, why a mother must, if need be, sacrifice all her other children in order to save the first-born; or why a daughter must sell her chastity to get funds to pay for the father's dissipation, and the like. Starting as Right Reason, *Giri* has, in my opinion, often stooped to casuistry. It has even degenerated into cowardly fear of censure. I might say of *Giri* what Scott wrote of patriotism, that "as it is the fairest, so it is often the most suspicious, mask of other feelings." Carried beyond or below Right Reason, *Giri* became a monstrous misnomer. It harbored under its wings every sort of sophistry and hypocrisy. It might easily have been turned into a nest of cowardice, if Bushido had not a keen and correct sense of courage, the spirit of daring and bearing.

CHAPTER 4

勇敢忍耐精神

Courage, the Spirit of Daring and Bearing

Courage was scarcely deemed worthy to be counted among virtues, unless it was exercised in the cause of Righteousness. In his *Analects* Confucius defines Courage by explaining, as is often his wont, what its negative is. "Perceiving what is right," he says, "and doing it not, argues lack of courage." Put this epigram into a positive statement, and it runs, "Courage is doing what is right." To run all kinds of hazards, to jeopardize one's self, to rush into the jaws of death—these are too often identified with Valor, and in the profession of arms such rashness of conduct—what Shakespeare calls, "valor misbegot"—is unjustly applauded; but not so in the Precepts of Knighthood. Death for a cause unworthy of dying for, was called a "dog's death." "To rush into the thick of battle and to be slain in it," says a Prince of Mito, "is easy enough, and the merest churl is equal to the task; but," he continues, "it is true courage to live when it is right to live, and to die only when it is right to die," and yet the Prince had not even heard of the name of Plato, who defines courage as "the knowledge of things that a man should fear and that he should not fear." A distinction which is made in the West between moral and physical courage has long been recognized among us. What samurai youth has not heard of "Great Valor" and the "Valor of a Villein?"

Valor, Fortitude, Bravery, Fearlessness, Courage, being the qualities of soul which appeal most easily to juvenile minds, and which can be trained by exercise and example, were, so to speak, the most popular virtues, early emulated among the youth. Stories of military exploits were repeated almost before boys left their mother's breast. Does a little booby cry for any ache? The mother scolds him in this fashion: "What a coward to cry

'The Earth Spider is Slain by Brave Samurai Watanabe no Tauna', by Katsukawa Shunshō (1726–92), colour woodblock print.

for a trifling pain! What will you do when your arm is cut off in battle? What when you are called upon to commit hara-kiri?" We all know the pathetic fortitude of a famished little boy-prince of Sendai, who in the drama is made to say to his little page, "Seest thou those tiny sparrows in the nest, how their yellow bills are opened wide, and now see! there comes their mother with worms to feed them. How eagerly and happily the little ones eat! but for a samurai, when his stomach is empty, it is a disgrace to feel hunger." Anecdotes of fortitude and bravery abound in nursery tales, though stories of this kind are not by any means the only method of early imbuing the spirit with daring and fearlessness. Parents, with sternness sometimes verging on cruelty, set their children to tasks that called forth all the pluck that was in them. "Bears hurl their cubs down the gorge," they said. Samurai's sons were let down the steep valleys of hardship, and spurred to Sisyphus-like tasks. Occasional deprivation of food or exposure to cold, was considered a highly efficacious test for inuring them to endurance. Children of tender age were sent among utter strangers with some message to deliver, were made to rise before the sun, and before breakfast attend to their reading exercises, walking to their teacher with bare feet in the cold of winter; they frequently—once or twice a month, as on the festival of a god of learning—came together in small groups and passed the night without sleep, in reading aloud by turns. Pilgrimages to all sorts of uncanny places—to execution grounds, to graveyards, to houses reputed to be haunted, were favorite pastimes of the young. In the days when decapitation was public, not only were small boys sent to witness the ghastly scene, but they were made to visit alone the place in the darkness of night and there to leave a mark of their visit on the trunkless head.

Does this ultra-Spartan system of "drilling the nerves" strike the modern pedagogist with horror and doubt—doubt whether the tendency would not be brutalizing, nipping in the bud the tender emotions of the heart? Let us see what other concepts Bushido had of Valor.

The spiritual aspect of valor is evidenced by composure—calm presence of mind. Tranquillity is courage in repose. It is a statical manifestation of valor, as daring deeds are a dynamical. A truly brave man is ever serene; he is never taken by surprise; nothing ruffles the equanimity of his spirit. In the heat of battle he remains cool; in the midst of catastrophes he keeps level his mind. Earthquakes do not shake him, he laughs at storms. We admire him as truly great, who, in the menacing presence of danger or death, retains his self-possession; who, for instance, can compose a poem under impending peril or hum a strain in the face of death. Such indulgence betraying no tremor in the writing or in the voice, is taken as an infallible index of a large nature—of what we call a capacious mind (*Yoyū*), which, for from being pressed or crowded, has always room for something more.

It passes current among us as a piece of authentic history, that as Ōta Dokan, the great builder of the castle of Tokyo, was pierced through with a spear, his assassin, knowing the poetical predilection of his victim, accompanied his thrust with this couplet:

"Ah! how in moments like these
Our heart doth grudge the light of life;"

Whereupon the expiring hero, not one whit daunted by the mortal wound in his side, added the lines:

"Had not in hours of peace,
It learned to lightly look on life."

There is even a sportive element in a courageous nature. Things which are serious to ordinary people, may be but play to the valiant. Hence in old warfare it was not at all rare for the parties to a conflict to exchange repartee or to begin a rhetorical contest. Combat was not solely a matter of brute force; it was, as, well, an intellectual engagement.

Of such character was the battle fought on the bank of the Koromo River, late in the eleventh century. The eastern army routed, its leader, Sadato, took to flight. When the pursuing general pressed him hard and called aloud—"It is a disgrace for a warrior to show his back to the enemy," Sadato reined his horse; upon this the conquering chief shouted an impromptu verse:

"Torn into shreds is the warp of the cloth" (*koromo*).

Scarcely had the words escaped his lips when the defeated warrior, undismayed, completed the couplet:

"Since age has worn its threads by use."

Yoshiie, whose bow had all the while been bent, suddenly unstrung it and turned away, leaving his prospective victim to do as he pleased. When asked the reason of his strange behavior, he replied that he could not bear to put to shame one who had kept his presence of mind while hotly pursued by his enemy.

The sorrow which overtook Antony and Octavius at the death of Brutus, has been the general experience of brave men. Kenshin, who fought for fourteen years with Shingen, when he heard of the latter's death, wept aloud at the loss of "the best of enemies." It was this same Kenshin who had set a noble example for all time, in his treatment of Shingen, whose provinces lay in a mountainous region quite away from the sea, and who had consequently depended upon the Hōjō provinces of the Tokaido for salt. The Hōjō prince wishing to weaken him, although not openly at war with him, had cut off from Shingen all traffic in this important article. Kenshin, hearing of his enemy's dilemma and able to obtain his salt from the coast of his own dominions, wrote Shingen that in his opinion the Hōjō lord had committed a very mean act, and that although he (Kenshin) was at war with him (Shingen) he had ordered his subjects to furnish him with plenty of salt—adding, "I do not fight with salt, but with the sword," affording more than a parallel to the words of Camillus, "We Romans do not fight with gold, but with iron." Nietzsche spoke for the samurai heart when he wrote, "You are to be proud of your enemy; then, the success of your enemy is your success also." Indeed valor and honor alike required that we should own as enemies in war only such as prove worthy of being friends in peace. When valor attains this height, it becomes akin to benevolence.

Uesugi Kenshin (1530–78) rides into battle. One of the most powerful daimyō *(warlord) of the Sengoku period, he was noted for his honorable conduct and military expertise.*

CHAPTER 5

仁、苦難

Benevolence, the Feeling of Distress

Love, magnanimity, affection for others, sympathy and pity, were ever recognized to be supreme virtues, the highest of all the attributes of the human soul. Benevolence was deemed a princely virtue in a twofold sense: princely among the manifold attributes of a noble spirit; princely as particularly befitting a princely profession. We needed no Shakespeare to feel—though, perhaps, like the rest of the world, we needed him to express it—that mercy became a monarch better than his crown, that it was above his sceptered sway. How often both Confucius and Mencius repeat the highest requirement of a ruler of men to consist in benevolence. Confucius would say, "Let but a prince cultivate virtue, people will flock to him; with people will come to him lands; lands will bring forth for him wealth; wealth will give him the benefit of right uses. Virtue is the root, and wealth an outcome." Again, "Never has there been a case of a sovereign loving benevolence, and the people not loving righteousness," Mencius follows close at his heels and says, "Instances are on record where individuals attained to supreme power in a single state, without benevolence, but never have I heard of a whole empire falling into the hands of one who lacked this virtue." Also, "It is impossible that anyone should become ruler of the people to whom they have not yielded the subjection of their hearts." Both defined this indispensable requirement in a ruler by saying, "Benevolence—Benevolence is Man." Under the régime of feudalism, which could easily be perverted into militarism, it was to Benevolence that we owed our deliverance from despotism of the worst kind. An utter surrender of "life and limb" on the part of the governed would have left nothing for the governing but self-will, and this has for its natural consequence the growth of that absolutism so often called "oriental despotism"—as though there were no despots of occidental history!

Head of the powerful Oda clan, Oda Nobunaga (1551–82) was a leading daimyō *(warlord) of the Sengoku period and considered the 'Great Unifier' of Japan.*

Uesugi Harunori (1751–1822) was the ninth daimyō *of Yonezawa domain and known for his good governance and financial skill.*

Let it be far from me to uphold despotism of any sort; but it is a mistake to identify feudalism with it. When Frederick the Great wrote that "Kings are the first servants of the State," jurists thought rightly that a new era was reached in the development of freedom. Strangely coinciding in time, in the backwoods of North-western Japan, Yozan of Yonézawa made exactly the same declaration, showing that feudalism was not all tyranny and oppression. A feudal prince, although unmindful of owing reciprocal obligations to his vassals, felt a higher sense of responsibility to his ancestors and to Heaven. He was a father to his subjects, whom Heaven entrusted to his care. In a sense not usually assigned to the term, Bushido accepted and corroborated paternal government—paternal also as opposed to the less interested avuncular government (Uncle Sam's, to wit!). The difference between a despotic and a paternal government lies in this, that in the one the people obey reluctantly, while in the other they do so with "that proud submission, that dignified obedience, that subordination of heart which kept alive, even in servitude itself, the spirit of exalted freedom."[8] The old saying is not entirely false which called the king of England the "king of devils, because of his subjects' often insurrections against, and depositions of, their princes," and which made the French monarch the "king of asses, because of their infinite taxes and Impositions," but which gave the title of "the king of men" to the sovereign of Spain "because of his subjects' willing obedience." But enough!

Virtue and absolute power may strike the Anglo-Saxon mind as terms which it is impossible to harmonize. Pobyedonostseff has clearly set before us the contrast in the foundations of English and other European communities; namely that these were organized on the basis of common interest, while that was distinguished by a strongly developed independent personality. What this Russian statesman says of the personal dependence of individuals on some social alliance and in the end of ends of the State, among the continental nations of Europe and particularly among Slavonic peoples, is doubly true of the Japanese. Hence not only is a free exercise of monarchical power not felt as heavily by us as in Europe, but it is generally moderated by parental consideration for the feelings of the people. "Absolutism," says Bismarck, "primarily demands in the ruler impartiality, honesty, devotion to duty, energy and inward humility." If I may be allowed to make one more quotation on this subject, I will cite

[8] Burke, *French Revolution*.

from the speech of the German Emperor at Coblenz, in which he spoke of "Kingship, by the grace of God, with its heavy duties, its tremendous responsibility to the Creator alone, from which no man, no minister, no parliament, can release the monarch."

We knew Benevolence was a tender virtue and mother-like. If upright Rectitude and stern Justice were peculiarly masculine, Mercy had the gentleness and the persuasiveness of a feminine nature. We were warned against indulging in indiscriminate charity, without seasoning it with justice and rectitude. Masamuné expressed it well in his oft-quoted aphorism—"Rectitude carried to excess hardens into stiffness; Benevolence indulged beyond measure sinks into weakness."

Fortunately Mercy was not so rare as it was beautiful, for it is universally true that "The bravest are the tenderest, the loving are the daring." "*Bushi no nasaké*"—the tenderness of a warrior—had a sound which appealed at once to whatever was noble in us; not that the mercy of a samurai was generically different from the mercy of any other being, but because it implied mercy where mercy was not a blind impulse, but where it recognized due regard to justice, and where mercy did not remain merely a certain state of mind, but where it was backed with power to save or kill. As economists speak of demand as being effectual or ineffectual, similarly we may call the mercy of *bushi* effectual, since it implied the power of acting for the good or detriment of the recipient.

Priding themselves as they did in their brute strength and privileges to turn it into account, the samurai gave full consent to what Mencius taught concerning the power of Love. "Benevolence," he says, "brings under its sway whatever hinders its power, just as water subdues fire: they only doubt the power of water to quench flames who try to extinguish with a cupful a whole burning wagon-load of faggots." He also says that "the feeling of distress is the root of benevolence, therefore a benevolent man is ever mindful of those who are suffering and in distress." Thus did Mencius long anticipate Adam Smith who founds his ethical philosophy on Sympathy.

It is indeed striking how closely the code of knightly honor of one country coincides with that of others; in other words, how the much

Samurai warriors Ichijo Jiro Tadanori and Notonokami Noritsune join in combat.

abused oriental ideas of morals find their counterparts in the noblest maxims of European literature. If the well-known lines,

Hae tibi erunt artes—pacisque imponere morem,
Parcere subjectis, et debellare superbos,

were shown a Japanese gentleman, he might readily accuse the Mantuan bard of plagiarizing from the literature of his own country. Benevolence to the weak, the downtrodden or the vanquished, was ever extolled as peculiarly becoming to a samurai. Lovers of Japanese art must be familiar with the representation of a priest riding backwards on a cow. The rider was once a warrior who in his day made his name a by-word of terror. In that terrible battle of Sumano-ura (1184 A.D.), which was one of the most decisive in our history, he overtook an enemy and in single combat had him in the clutch of his gigantic arms. Now the etiquette of war required that on such occasions no blood should be spilt, unless the weaker party proved to be a man of rank or ability equal to that of the stronger. The grim combatant would have the name of the man under him; but he refusing to make it known, his helmet was ruthlessly torn off, when the sight of a juvenile face, fair and beardless, made the astonished knight relax his hold. Helping the youth to his feet, in paternal tones he bade the stripling go: "Off, young prince, to thy mother's side! The sword of Kumagaye shall never be tarnished by a drop of thy blood. Haste and flee o'er yon pass before thy enemies come in sight!" The young warrior refused to go and begged Kumagaye, for the honor of both, to despatch him on the spot. Above the hoary head of the veteran gleams the cold blade, which many a time before has sundered the chords of life, but his stout heart quails; there flashes athwart his mental eye the vision of his own boy, who this self-same day marched to the sound of bugle to try his maiden arms; the strong hand of the warrior quivers; again he begs his victim to flee for his life. Finding all his entreaties vain and hearing the approaching steps of his comrades, he exclaims: "If thou art overtaken, thou mayest fall at a more ignoble hand than mine. O, thou Infinite! receive his soul!" In an instant the sword flashes in the air, and when it falls it is red with adolescent blood. When the war is ended, we find our soldier returning in triumph, but little cares he now for honor or fame; he renounces his warlike career, shaves his head, dons a priestly garb, devotes the rest of his days to holy pilgrimage, never turning his back to the West, where lies the Paradise whence salvation comes and whither the sun hastes daily for his rest.

Critics may point out flaws in this story, which is casuistically vulnerable. Let it be: all the same it shows that Tenderness, Pity and Love, were traits which adorned the most sanguinary exploits of the samurai. It was an old maxim among them that "It becometh not the fowler to slay the bird which takes refuge in his bosom." This in a large measure explains why the Red Cross movement, considered peculiarly Christian, so readily found a firm footing among us. For decades before we heard of the Geneva Convention, Bakin, our greatest novelist, had familiarized us with the medical treatment of a fallen foe. In the principality of Satsuma, noted for its martial spirit and education, the custom prevailed for young men to practice music; not the blast of trumpets or the beat of drums—"those clamorous harbingers of blood and death"—stirring us to imitate the actions of a tiger, but sad and tender melodies on the *biwa*,[9] soothing our fiery spirits, drawing our thoughts away from scent of blood and scenes of carnage. Polybius tells us of the Constitution of Arcadia, which required all youths under thirty to practice music, in order that this gentle art might alleviate the rigors of that inclement region. It is to its influence that he attributes the absence of cruelty in that part of the Arcadian mountains.

Nor was Satsuma the only place in Japan where gentleness was inculcated among the warrior class. A Prince of Shirakawa jots down his random thoughts, and among them is the following: "Though they come stealing to your bedside in the silent watches of the night, drive not away, but rather cherish these—the fragrance of flowers, the sound of distant bells, the insect humming of a frosty night." And again, "Though they may wound your feelings, these three you have only to forgive, the breeze that scatters your flowers, the cloud that hides your moon, and the man who tries to pick quarrels with you."

It was ostensibly to express, but actually to cultivate, these gentler emotions that the writing of verses was encouraged. Our poetry has

[9] A musical instrument, resembling the guitar.

therefore a strong undercurrent of pathos and tenderness. A well-known anecdote of a rustic samurai illustrates a case in point. When he was told to learn versification, and "The Warbler's Notes" was given him for the subject of his first attempt, his fiery spirit rebelled and he *flung* at the feet of his master this uncouth production, which ran:

"The brave warrior keeps apart
The ear that might listen
To the warbler's song."

His master, undaunted by the crude sentiment, continued to encourage the youth, until one day the music of his soul was awakened to respond to the sweet notes of the *uguisu*,[10] and he wrote:

"Stands the warrior, mailed and strong,
To hear the uguisu's song,
Warbled sweet the trees among."

We admire and enjoy the heroic incident in Körner's short life, when, as he lay wounded on the battle-field, he scribbled his famous "Farewell to Life." Incidents of a similar kind were not at all unusual in our warfare. Our pithy, epigrammatic poems were particularly well suited to the improvisation of a single sentiment. Everybody of any education was either a poet or a poetaster. Not infrequently a marching soldier might be seen to halt, take his writing utensils from his belt, and compose an ode—and such papers were found afterward in the helmets or the breast-plates, when these were removed from their lifeless wearers.

What Christianity has done in Europe toward rousing compassion in the midst of belligerent horrors, love of music and letters has done in Japan. The cultivation of tender feelings breeds considerate regard for the sufferings of others. Modesty and complaisance, actuated by respect for others' feelings, are at the root of politeness.

[10] The *uguisu* or warbler, sometimes called the nightingale of Japan.

'Warbler on a Plum Branch', by Utagawa Hiroshige (c. 1835).

CHAPTER 6

礼儀正しさ

Politeness

Courtesy and urbanity of manners has been noticed by every foreign tourist as a marked Japanese trait. Politeness is a poor virtue, if it is actuated only by a fear of offending good taste, whereas it should be the outward manifestation of a sympathetic regard for the feelings of others. It also implies a due regard for the fitness of things, therefore due respect to social positions; for these latter express no plutocratic distinctions, but were originally distinctions for actual merit.

In its highest form, politeness almost approaches love. We may reverently say, politeness "suffereth long, and is kind; envieth not, vaunteth not itself, is not puffed up; doth not behave itself unseemly, seeketh not her own, is not easily provoked, taketh not account of evil." Is it any wonder that Professor Dean, in speaking of the six elements of Humanity, accords to Politeness an exalted position, inasmuch as it is the ripest fruit of social intercourse?

While thus extolling Politeness, far be it from me to put it in the front rank of virtues. If we analyze it, we shall find it correlated with other virtues of a higher order; for what virtue stands alone? While—or rather because—it was exalted as peculiar to the profession of arms, and as such esteemed in a degree higher than its deserts, there came into existence its counterfeits. Confucius himself has repeatedly taught that external appurtenances are as little a part of propriety as sounds are of music.

When propriety was elevated to the *sine qua non* of social intercourse, it was only to be expected that an elaborate system of

'Samurai Admiring Pine-Tree and Plum Blossoms', by Ryūryūkyo Shinsai (1799–1823).

'Southern Barbarian screens', showing Europeans landing on Japanese shores in the early seventeenth century.

etiquette should come into vogue to train youth in correct social behavior. How one must bow in accosting others, how he must walk and sit, were taught and learned with utmost care. Table manners grew to be a science. Tea serving and drinking were raised to a ceremony. A man of education is, of course, expected to be master of all these. Very fitly does Mr. Veblen, in his interesting book,[11] call decorum "a product and an exponent of the leisure-class life."

I have heard slighting remarks made by Europeans upon our elaborate discipline of politeness. It has been criticized as absorbing too much of our thought and in so far a folly to observe strict obedience to it. I admit that there may be unnecessary niceties in ceremonious etiquette, but whether it partakes as much of folly as the adherence to ever-changing fashions of the West, is a question not very clear to my mind. Even fashions I do not consider solely as freaks of vanity; on the contrary, I look upon these as a ceaseless search of the human mind for the beautiful. Much less do I consider elaborate ceremony as altogether trivial; for it denotes the result of long observation as to the most appropriate method of achieving a certain result. If there is anything to do, there is certainly a best way to do it, and the best way is both the most economical and the most graceful. Mr. Spencer defines grace as the most economical manner of motion. The tea ceremony presents certain definite ways of manipulating a bowl, a spoon, a napkin, etc. To a novice it looks tedious. But one soon discovers that the way prescribed is, after all, the most saving of time and labor; in other words, the most economical use of force—hence, according to Spencer's dictum, the most graceful.

The spiritual significance of social decorum—or, I might say, to borrow from the vocabulary of the "Philosophy of Clothes," the spiritual discipline of which etiquette and ceremony are mere outward garments—is out of all proportion to what their appearance warrants us in believing. I might follow the example of Mr. Spencer and trace in our ceremonial institutions their origins and the moral motives that gave rise to them; but that is not what I shall endeavor to do in this book. It is the moral training involved in strict observance of propriety, that I wish to emphasize.

[11] *Theory of the Leisure Class,* N.Y. 1899, p. 46.

'Osen Waiting on a Young Samurai', by Suzuki Harunobu (c. 1770).

I have said that etiquette was elaborated into the finest niceties, so much so that different schools advocating different systems, came into existence. But they all united in the ultimate essential, and this was put by a great exponent of the best known school of etiquette, the Ogasawara, in the following terms: "The end of all etiquette is to so cultivate your mind that even when you are quietly seated, not the roughest ruffian can dare make onset on your person." It means, in other words, that by constant exercise in correct manners, one brings all the parts and faculties of his body into perfect order and into such harmony with itself and its environment as to express the mastery of spirit over the flesh. What a new and deep significance the French word *biensèance*[12] comes thus to contain!

If the premise is true that gracefulness means economy of force, then it follows as a logical sequence that a constant practice of graceful deportment must bring with it a reserve and storage of force. Fine manners, therefore, mean power in repose. When the barbarian Gauls, during the sack of Rome, burst into the assembled Senate and dared pull the beards of the venerable Fathers, we think the old gentlemen were to blame, inasmuch as they lacked dignity and strength of manners. Is lofty spiritual attainment really possible through etiquette? Why not? All roads lead to Rome!

As an example of how the simplest thing can be made into an art and then become spiritual culture, I may take *Cha-no-yu*, the tea ceremony. Tea-sipping as a fine art! Why should it not be? In the children drawing pictures on the sand, or in the savage carving on a rock, was the promise of a Raphael or a Michael Angelo. How much more is the drinking of a beverage, which began with the transcendental contemplation of a Hindoo anchorite, entitled to develop into a handmaid of Religion and Morality? That calmness of mind, that serenity of temper, that composure and quietness of demeanor, which are the first essentials of *Cha-no-yu,* are without doubt the first conditions of right thinking and right feeling. The scrupulous cleanliness of the little room, shut off from sight and sound of the madding crowd, is in itself conducive to direct one's thoughts from the world. The bare interior does not engross one's attention like the innumerable pictures and bric-à-brac of a Western

[12] Etymologically *well-seatedness.*

parlor; the presence of *kakemono*[13] calls our attention more to grace of design than to beauty of color. The utmost refinement of taste is the object aimed at; whereas anything like display is banished with religious horror. The very fact that it was invented by a contemplative recluse, in a time when wars and the rumors of wars were incessant, is well calculated to show that this institution was more than a pastime. Before entering the quiet precincts of the tea-room, the company assembling to partake of the ceremony laid aside, together with their swords, the ferocity of the battlefield or the cares of government, there to find peace and friendship.

Cha-no-yu is more than a ceremony—it is a fine art; it is poetry, with articulate gestures for rhythm: it is a *modus operandi* of soul discipline. Its greatest value lies in this last phase. Not infrequently the other phases preponderated in the mind of its votaries, but that does not prove that its essence was not of a spiritual nature.

Politeness will be a great acquisition, if it does no more than impart grace to manners; but its function does not stop here. For propriety, springing as it does from motives of benevolence and modesty, and actuated by tender feelings toward the sensibilities of others, is ever a graceful expression of sympathy. Its requirement is that we should weep with those that weep and rejoice with those that rejoice. Such didactic requirement, when reduced into small every-day details of life, expresses itself in little acts scarcely noticeable, or, if noticed, is, as one missionary lady of twenty years' residence once said to me, "awfully funny." You are out in the hot glaring sun with no shade over you; a Japanese acquaintance passes by; you accost him, and instantly his hat is off—well, that is perfectly natural, but the "awfully funny" performance is, that all the while he talks with you his parasol is down and he stands in the glaring sun also. How foolish!—Yes, exactly so, provided the motive were less than this: "You are in the sun; I sympathize with you; I would willingly take you under my parasol if it were large enough, or if we were familiarly acquainted; as I cannot shade you, I will share your discomforts." Little acts of this kind, equally or more amusing, are not mere gestures or conventionalities. They are the "bodying forth" of thoughtful feelings for the comfort of others.

[13] Hanging scrolls, which may be either paintings or ideograms, used for decorative purposes.

Sen no Rikyū (1522–91), is considered the historical figure with the most profound influence on chanoyu, *the Japanese 'Way of Tea'.*

Another "awfully funny" custom is dictated by our canons of Politeness; but many superficial writers on Japan, have dismissed it by simply attributing it to the general topsy-turvyness of the nation. Every foreigner who has observed it will confess the awkwardness he felt in making proper reply upon the occasion. In America, when you make a gift, you sing its praises to the recipient; in Japan we depreciate or slander it. The underlying idea with you is, "This is a nice gift: if it were not nice I would not dare give it to you; for it will be an insult to give you anything but what is nice." In contrast to this, our logic runs: "You are a nice person, and no gift is nice enough for you. You will not accept anything I can lay at your feet except as a token of my good will; so accept this, not for its intrinsic value, but as a token. It will be an insult to your worth to call the best gift good enough for you." Place the two ideas side by side; and we see that the ultimate idea is one and the same. Neither is "awfully funny." The American speaks of the material which makes the gift; the Japanese speaks of the spirit which prompts the gift.

It is perverse reasoning to conclude, because our sense of propriety shows itself in all the smallest ramifications of our deportment, to take the least important of them and uphold it as the type, and pass judgment upon the principle itself. Which is more important, to eat or to observe rules of propriety about eating? A Chinese sage answers, "If you take a case where the eating is all-important, and the observing the rules of propriety is of little importance, and compare them together, why merely say that the eating is of the more importance?" "Metal is heavier than feathers," but does that saying have reference to a single clasp of metal and a wagon-load of feathers? Take a piece of wood a foot thick and raise it above the pinnacle of a temple, none would call it taller than the temple. To the question, "Which is the more important, to tell the truth or to be polite?" the Japanese are said to give an answer diametrically opposite to what the American will say—but I forbear any comment until I come to speak of veracity, or truthfulness.

The young samurai Rikiya places a gift in front of Konami with her mother behind her, from Act Two of the Chūshingura*, a fictionalised account of the 47* rōnin *and their mission to avenge the death of their master, Asano Naganori.*

CHAPTER 7

真偽

Veracity or Truthfulness

Without veracity and sincerity, politeness is a farce and a show. "Propriety carried beyond right bounds," says Masamuné, "becomes a lie." An ancient poet has outdone Polonius in the advice he gives: "To thyself be faithful: if in thy heart thou strayest not from truth, without prayer of thine the Gods will keep thee whole." The apotheosis of Sincerity to which Tsu-tsu gives expression in the *Doctrine of the Mean*, attributes to it transcendental powers, almost identifying them with the Divine. "Sincerity is the end and the beginning of all things; without Sincerity there would be nothing." He then dwells with eloquence on its far-reaching and long enduring nature, its power to produce changes without movement and by its mere presence to accomplish its purpose without effort. From the Chinese ideogram for Sincerity, which is a combination of "Word" and "Perfect," one is tempted to draw a parallel between it and the Neo-Platonic doctrine of *Logos*—to such height does the sage soar in his unwonted mystic flight.

Lying or equivocation were deemed equally cowardly. The *bushi* held that his high social position demanded a loftier standard of veracity than that of the tradesman and peasant. *Bushi no ichi-gon*—the word of a samurai or in exact German equivalent *ein Ritterwort*—was sufficient guaranty of the truthfulness of an assertion. His word carried such weight with it that promises were generally made and fulfilled without a written pledge, which would have been deemed quite beneath his dignity. Many thrilling anecdotes were told of those who atoned by death for *ni-gon*, a double tongue.

The great Chinese sage Zisi, born Kong Ji (c. 481–402 BCE), was a grandson of Confucius and passed on Confucian teaching to Mencius (Mengzi).

The regard for veracity was so high that, unlike the generality of Christians who persistently violate the plain commands of the Teacher not to swear, the best of samurai looked upon an oath as derogatory to their honor. I am well aware that they did swear by different deities or upon their swords; but never has swearing degenerated into wanton form and irreverent interjection. To emphasize our words a practice of literally sealing with blood was sometimes resorted to. For the explanation of such a practice, I need only refer my readers to Goethe's *Faust*.

A recent American writer is responsible for this statement, that if you ask an ordinary Japanese which is better, to tell a falsehood or be impolite, he will not hesitate to answer "to tell a falsehood!" Dr. Peery[14] is partly right and partly wrong; right in that an ordinary Japanese, even a samurai, may answer in the way ascribed to him, but wrong in attributing too much weight to the term he translates "falsehood." This word (in Japanese *uso*) is employed to denote anything which is not a truth (*makoto*) or fact (*honto*). Lowell tells us that Wordsworth could not distinguish between truth and fact, and an ordinary Japanese is in this respect as good as Wordsworth. Ask a Japanese, or even an American of any refinement, to tell you whether he dislikes you or whether he is sick at his stomach, and he will not hesitate long to tell falsehoods and answer, "I like you much," or, "I am quite well, thank you." To sacrifice truth merely for the sake of politeness was regarded as an "empty form" (*kyo-rei*) and "deception by sweet words," and was never justified.

I own I am speaking now of the Bushido idea of veracity; but it may not be amiss to devote a few words to our commercial integrity, of which I have heard much complaint in foreign books and journals. A loose business morality has indeed been the worst blot on our national reputation; but before abusing it or hastily condemning the whole race for it, let us calmly study it and we shall be rewarded with consolation for the future.

Of all the great occupations of life, none was farther removed from the profession of arms than commerce. The merchant was placed lowest in the category of vocations—the knight, the tiller

[14] Peery, *The Gist of Japan*, p. 86.

'Onoe Matsusuke I as an Oiran Stands at the Left, Talking to Nakamura', by Torii Kiyonaga (c. 1788).

of the soil, the mechanic, the merchant. The samurai derived his income from land and could even indulge, if he had a mind to, in amateur farming; but the counter and abacus were abhorred. We knew the wisdom of this social arrangement. Montesquieu has made it clear that the debarring of the nobility from mercantile pursuits was an admirable social policy, in that it prevented wealth from accumulating in the hands of the powerful. The separation of power and riches kept the distribution of the latter more nearly equable. Professor Dill, the author of "Roman Society in the Last Century of the Western Empire," has brought afresh to our mind that one cause of the decadence of the Roman Empire, was the permission given to the nobility to engage in trade, and the consequent monopoly of wealth and power by a minority of the senatorial families.

Commerce, therefore, in feudal Japan did not reach that degree of development which it would have attained under freer conditions. The obloquy attached to the calling naturally brought within its pale such as cared little for social repute. "Call one a thief and he will steal:" put a stigma on a calling and its followers adjust their morals to it, for it is natural that "the normal conscience," as Hugh Black says, "rises to the demands made on it, and easily falls to the limit of the standard expected from it." It is unnecessary to add that no business, commercial or otherwise, can be transacted without a code of morals. Our merchants of the feudal period had one among themselves, without which they could never have developed, as they did, such fundamental mercantile institutions as the guild, the bank, the bourse, insurance, checks, bills of exchange, etc.; but in their relations with people outside their vocation, the tradesmen lived too true to the reputation of their order.

This being the case, when the country was opened to foreign trade, only the most adventurous and unscrupulous rushed to the ports, while the respectable business houses declined for some time the repeated requests of the authorities to establish branch houses. Was Bushido powerless to stay the current of commercial dishonor? Let us see.

Those who are well acquainted with our history will remember that only a few years after our treaty ports were opened to foreign

Ukie kinryuzan ichi no zu *('Perspective picture of the market at Kinryuzan Temple') by Toyokuni Utagawa (1769–1825). This artist's print shows a large throng of people at the open-air marketplace at Kinryuzan.*

trade, feudalism was abolished, and when with it the samurai's fiefs were taken and bonds issued to them in compensation, they were given liberty to invest them in mercantile transactions. Now you may ask, "Why could they not bring their much boasted veracity into their new business relations and so reform the old abuses?" Those who had eyes to see could not weep enough, those who had hearts to feel could not sympathize enough, with the fate of many a noble and honest samurai who signally and irrevocably failed in his new and unfamiliar field of trade and industry, through sheer lack of shrewdness in coping with his artful plebeian rival. When we know that eighty per cent of the business houses fail in so industrial a country as America, is it any wonder that scarcely one among a hundred samurai who went into trade could succeed in his new vocation? It will be long before it will be recognized how many fortunes were wrecked in the attempt to apply Bushido ethics to business methods; but it was soon patent to every observing mind that the ways of wealth were not the ways of honor. In what respects, then, were they different?

Of the three incentives to Veracity that Lecky enumerates, viz: the industrial, the political, and the philosophical, the first was altogether lacking in Bushido. As to the second, it could develop little in a political community under a feudal system. It is in its philosophical, and as Lecky says, in its highest aspect, that Honesty attained elevated rank in our catalogue of virtues. With all my sincere regard for the high commercial integrity of the Anglo-Saxon race, when I ask for the ultimate ground, I am told that "Honesty is the best policy," that it *pays* to be honest. Is not this virtue, then, its own reward? If it is followed because it brings in more cash than falsehood, I am afraid Bushido would rather indulge in lies!

If Bushido rejects a doctrine of *quid pro quo* rewards, the shrewder tradesman will readily accept it. Lecky has very truly remarked that Veracity owes its growth largely to commerce and manufacture; as Nietzsche puts it, "Honesty is the youngest of virtues"—in other words, it is the foster-child of industry, of modern industry. Without this mother, Veracity was like a blue-blood orphan whom only the most cultivated mind could adopt and nourish. Such minds were general among the samurai, but, for want of a more democratic and utilitarian foster-mother, the tender child failed to thrive. Industries advancing, Veracity will prove an easy, nay, a profitable, virtue to practice. Just think, as late as November 1880, Bismarck sent a circular to the professional consuls of the German Empire, warning them of "a lamentable lack of reliability with regard to German shipments *inter alia*, apparent both as to quality and quantity;" now-a-days we hear comparatively little of German carelessness and dishonesty in trade. In twenty years her merchants learned that in the end honesty pays. Already our merchants are finding that out. For the rest I recommend the reader to two recent writers for well-weighed judgment on this point.[15] It is interesting to remark in this connection that integrity and honor were the surest guaranties which even a merchant debtor could present in the form of promissory notes. It was quite a usual thing to insert such clauses as these: "In default of the repayment of the sum lent to me, I shall say nothing against being ridiculed in public;" or, "In case I fail to pay you back, you may call me a fool," and the like.

Often have I wondered whether the veracity of Bushido had any motive higher than courage. In the absence of any positive commandment against bearing false witness, lying was not condemned as sin, but simply denounced as weakness, and, as such, highly dishonorable. As a matter of fact, the idea of honesty is so intimately blended, and its Latin and its German etymology so identified with honor, that it is high time I should pause a few moments for the consideration of this feature of the Precepts of Knighthood.

[15] Knapp, *Feudal and Modern Japan*, Vol. I, Ch. IV. Ransome, *Japan in Transition*, Ch. VIII.

CHAPTER 8

名誉

Honor

The sense of honor, implying a vivid consciousness of personal dignity and worth, could not fail to characterize the samurai, born and bred to value the duties and privileges of their profession. Though the word ordinarily given nowadays as the translation of Honor was not used freely, yet the idea was conveyed by such terms as *na* (name), *men-moku* (countenance), *guai-bun* (outside hearing), reminding us respectively of the biblical use of "name," of the evolution of the term "personality" from the Greek mask, and of "fame." A good name—one's reputation, the immortal part of one's self, what remains being bestial—assumed as a matter of course, any infringement upon its integrity was felt as shame, and the sense of shame (*Ren-chi-shin*) was one of the earliest to be cherished in juvenile education. "You will be laughed at," "It will disgrace you," "Are you not ashamed?" were the last appeal to correct behavior on the part of a youthful delinquent. Such a recourse to his honor touched the most sensitive spot in the child's heart, as though it had been nursed on honor while it was in its mother's womb; for most truly is honor a prenatal influence, being closely bound up with strong family consciousness. "In losing the solidarity of families," says Balzac, "society has lost the fundamental force which Montesquieu named Honor." Indeed, the sense of shame seems to me to be the earliest indication of the moral consciousness of our race. The first and worst punishment which befell humanity in consequence of tasting "the fruit of that forbidden tree" was, to my mind, not the sorrow of childbirth, nor the thorns and thistles, but the awakening of the sense of shame. Few incidents in history excel in pathos the scene of the first mother plying with heaving breast and tremulous fingers, her crude needle

'Portrait of a Warrior', late sixteenth century. The unnamed samurai, clearly an important member of a warrior clan, grasps the end of his long beard—a feature banned in the seventeenth century as an expression of antiestablishment sentiment.

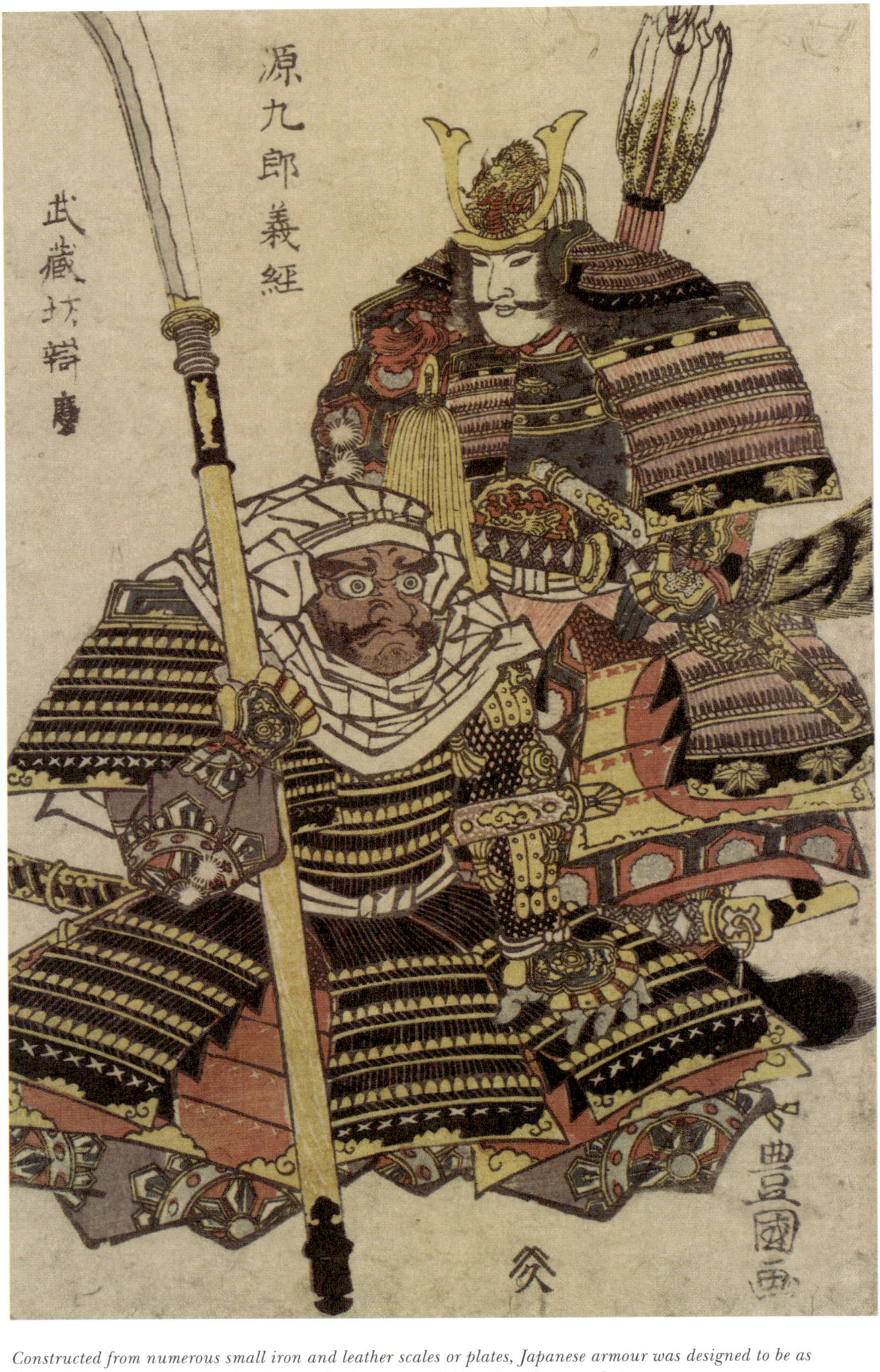

Constructed from numerous small iron and leather scales or plates, Japanese armour was designed to be as lightweight as possible, allowing the warrior to move quickly and easily in combat.

on the few fig leaves which her dejected husband plucked for her. This first fruit of disobedience clings to us with a tenacity that nothing else does. All the sartorial ingenuity of mankind has not yet succeeded in sewing an apron that will efficaciously hide our sense of shame. That samurai was right who refused to compromise his character by a slight humiliation in his youth; "because," he said, "dishonor is like a scar on a tree, which time, instead of effacing, only helps to enlarge."

Mencius had taught centuries before, in almost the identical phrase, what Carlyle has latterly expressed—namely, that "Shame is the soil of all Virtue, of good manners and good morals."

The fear of disgrace was so great that if our literature lacks such eloquence as Shakespeare puts into the mouth of Norfolk, it nevertheless hung like Damocles' sword over the head of every samurai and often assumed a morbid character. In the name of Honor, deeds were perpetrated which can find no justification in the code of Bushido. At the slightest, nay, imaginary insult, the quick-tempered braggart took offense, resorted to the use of the sword, and many an unnecessary strife was raised and many an innocent life lost. The story of a well-meaning citizen who called the attention of a *bushi* to a flea jumping on his back, and who was forthwith cut in two, for the simple and questionable reason that inasmuch as fleas are parasites which feed on animals, it was an unpardonable insult to identify a noble warrior with a beast—I say, stories like these are too frivolous to believe. Yet, the circulation of such stories implies three things: (1) that they were invented to overawe common people; (2) that abuses were really made of the samurai's profession of honor; and (3) that a very strong sense of shame was developed among them. It is plainly unfair to take an abnormal case to cast blame upon the Precepts, any more than to judge of the true teaching of Christ from the fruits of religious fanaticism and extravagance—inquisitions and hypocrisy. But, as in religious monomania there is something touchingly noble, as compared with the delirium tremens of a drunkard, so in that extreme sensitiveness of the samurai about their honor do we not recognize the substratum of a genuine virtue?

The morbid excess into which the delicate code of honor was inclined to run was strongly counterbalanced by preaching magnanimity and patience. To take offense at slight provocation was

ridiculed as "short-tempered." The popular adage said: "To bear what you think you cannot bear is really to bear." The great Iyéyasu left to posterity a few maxims, among which are the following: "The life of man is like going a long distance with a heavy load upon the shoulders. Haste not. ... Reproach none, but be forever watchful of thine own short-comings. ... Forbearance is the basis of length of days." He proved in his life what he preached. A literary wit put a characteristic epigram into the mouths of three well-known personages in our history: to Nobunaga he attributed, "I will kill her, if the nightingale sings not in time;" to Hidéyoshi, "I will force her to sing for me;" and to Iyéyasu, "I will wait till she opens her lips."

Patience and long suffering were also highly commended by Mencius. In one place he writes to this effect: "Though you denude yourself and insult me, what is that to me? You cannot defile my soul by your outrage." Elsewhere he teaches that anger at a petty offense is unworthy of a superior man, but indignation for a great cause is righteous wrath.

To what height of unmartial and unresisting meekness Bushido could reach in some of its votaries, may be seen in their utterances. Take, for instance, this saying of Ogawa: "When others speak all manner of evil things against thee, return not evil for evil, but rather reflect that thou wast not more faithful in the discharge of thy duties." Take another of Kumazawa: "When others blame thee, blame them not; when others are angry at thee, return not anger. Joy cometh only as Passion and Desire part." Still another instance I may cite from Saigo, upon whose overhanging brows "shame is ashamed to sit"—"The Way is the way of Heaven and Earth: Man's place is to follow it: therefore make it the object of thy life to reverence Heaven. Heaven loves me and others with equal love; therefore with the love wherewith thou lovest thyself, love others. Make not Man thy partner but Heaven, and making Heaven thy partner do thy best. Never condemn others; but see to it that thou comest not short of thine own mark." Some of those sayings remind us of Christian expostulations and show us how far in practical morality natural religion can approach the revealed. Not only did these sayings remain as utterances, but they were really embodied in acts.

It must be admitted that very few attained this sublime height of magnanimity, patience and forgiveness. It was a great pity that nothing

Actor Sawamura Tosshō ((1838–86), half-length portrait, in the role of Shirai Gonpachi, a samurai turned outlaw, about to draw his sword.

clear and general was expressed as to what constitutes Honor, only a few enlightened minds being aware that it "from no condition rises," but that it lies in each acting well his part: for nothing was easier than for youths to forget in the heat of action what they had learned in Mencius in their calmer moments. Said this sage, "'Tis in every man's mind to love honor: but little doth he dream that what is truly honorable lies within himself and not anywhere else. The honor which men confer is not good honor. Those whom Châo the Great ennobles, he can make mean again."

For the most part, an insult was quickly resented and repaid by death, as we shall see later, while Honor—too often nothing higher than vain glory or worldly approbation—was prized as the *summum bonum* of earthly existence. Fame, and not wealth or knowledge, was the goal toward which youths had to strive. Many a lad swore within himself as he crossed the threshold of his paternal home, that he would not recross it until he had made a name in the world: and many an ambitious mother refused to see her sons again unless they could "return home," as the expression is, "caparisoned in brocade." To shun shame or win a name, samurai boys would submit to any privations and undergo severest ordeals of bodily or mental suffering. They knew that honor won in youth grows with age. In the memorable siege of Osaka, a young son of Iyéyasu, in spite of his earnest entreaties to be put in the vanguard, was placed at the rear of the army. When the castle fell, he was so chagrined and wept so bitterly that an old councillor tried to console him with all the resources at his command. "Take comfort, Sire," said he, "at thought of the long future before you. In the many years that you may live, there will come divers occasions to distinguish yourself." The boy fixed his indignant gaze upon the man and said—"How foolishly you talk! Can ever my fourteenth year come round again?"

Life itself was thought cheap if honor and fame could be attained therewith: hence, whenever a cause presented itself which was considered dearer than life, with utmost serenity and celerity was life laid down.

Of the causes in comparison with which no life was too dear to sacrifice, was the duty of loyalty, which was the key-stone that made feudal virtues a symmetrical arch.

This triptych illustrates an episode from the life of the popular hero Yoshitsune (1159–89), who was also known as Ushiwaka-maru *(young ox). On one of his nightly outings from the temple, 12-year-old Yoshitsune encountered Benkei on the Gojo Bridge in Kyoto. Benkei, a wild giant of a man, had been told by a swordsmith that he could forge a magic sword from the tips and cutting edges of a thousand blades. He obtained the swords by attacking samurai warriors crossing the Gojo Bridge.*

CHAPTER 9

忠誠

The Duty of Loyalty

Other virtues feudal morality shares in common with other systems of ethics, with other classes of people, but this virtue—homage and fealty to a superior—is its distinctive feature. I am aware that personal fidelity is a moral adhesion existing among all sorts and conditions of men—a gang of pickpockets owe allegiance to a Fagin; but it is only in the code of chivalrous honor that Loyalty assumes paramount importance.

In spite of Hegel's criticism that the fidelity of feudal vassals, being an obligation to an individual and not to a Commonwealth, is a bond established on totally unjust principles,[16] a great compatriot of his made it his boast that personal loyalty was a German virtue. Bismarck had good reason to do so, not because the *Treue* he boasts of was the monopoly of his Fatherland or of any single nation or race, but because this favored fruit of chivalry lingers latest among the people where feudalism has lasted longest. In America where "everybody is as good as anybody else," and, as the Irishman added, "better too," such exalted ideas of loyalty as we feel for our sovereign may be deemed "excellent within certain bounds," but preposterous as encouraged among us. Montesquieu complained long ago that right on one side of the Pyrenees was wrong on the other, and the recent Dreyfus trial proved the truth of his remark, save that the Pyrenees were not the sole boundary beyond which French justice finds no accord. Similarly, Loyalty as we conceive it may find few admirers elsewhere, not because our conception is wrong, but because it is, I am afraid, forgotten, and also because we carry it to

[16] *Philosophy of History* (Eng. trans. by Sibree), Pt. IV, Sec. II, Ch. I.

Kamakura no Koshi ('The Filial Son at Kamakura'), from a woodblock print, c. 1835.

'Sugawara Michizane in Exile', by Kobayashi Kiyochika, 1884.

a degree not reached in any other country. Griffis[17] was quite right in stating that whereas in China Confucian ethics made obedience to parents the primary human duty, in Japan precedence was given to Loyalty. At the risk of shocking some of my good readers, I will relate of one "who could endure to follow a fall'n lord" and who thus, as Shakespeare assures, "earned a place i' the story."

The story is of one of the purest characters in our history, Michizané, who, falling a victim to jealousy and calumny, is exiled from the capital. Not content with this, his unrelenting enemies are now bent upon the extinction of his family. Strict search for his son—not yet grown—reveals the fact of his being secreted in a village school kept by one Genzo, a former vassal of Michizané. When orders are dispatched to the schoolmaster to deliver the head of the juvenile offender on a certain day, his first idea is to find a suitable substitute for it. He ponders over his school-list, scrutinizes with careful eyes all the boys, as they stroll into the classroom, but none among the children born of the soil bears the least resemblance to his protégé. His despair, however, is but for a moment; for, behold, a new scholar is announced—a comely boy of the same age as his master's son, escorted by a mother of noble mien. No less conscious of the resemblance between infant lord and infant retainer, were the mother and the boy himself. In the privacy of home both had laid themselves upon the altar; the one his life—the other her heart, yet without sign to the outer world. Unwitting of what had passed between them, it is the teacher from whom comes the suggestion.

Here, then, is the scape-goat! The rest of the narrative may be briefly told. On the day appointed, arrives the officer commissioned to identify and receive the head of the youth. Will he be deceived by the false head? The poor Genzo's hand is on the hilt of the sword, ready to strike a blow either at the man or at himself, should the examination defeat his scheme. The officer takes up the gruesome object before him, goes calmly over each feature, and in a deliberate, business-like tone, pronounces it genuine. That evening in a lonely home awaits the mother we saw in the school. Does she know the fate of her child? It is not for his return that she watches with eagerness for the opening of the wicket. Her father-in-law has been for a long

[17] *Religions of Japan.*

Taira no Kiyomori (1118–81) sits among his books, while in front of him his son Shigemori (1138–79) pays his respects.

time a recipient of Michizané's bounties, but since his banishment circumstances have forced her husband to follow the service of the enemy of his family's benefactor. He himself could not be untrue to his own cruel master; but his son could serve the cause of the grandsire's lord. As one acquainted with the exile's family, it was he who had been entrusted with the task of identifying the boy's head. Now the day's—yea, the life's—hard work is done, he returns home and as he crosses its threshold, he accosts his wife, saying: "Rejoice, my wife, our darling son has proved of service to his lord!"

"What an atrocious story!" I hear my readers exclaim, "Parents deliberately sacrificing their own innocent child to save the life of another man's." But this child was a conscious and willing victim: it is a story of vicarious death—as significant as, and not more revolting than, the story of Abraham's intended sacrifice of Isaac. In both cases it was obedience to the call of duty, utter submission to the command of a higher voice, whether given by a visible or an invisible angel, or heard by an outward or an inward ear; but I abstain from preaching.

The individualism of the West, which recognizes separate interests for father and son, husband and wife, necessarily brings into strong relief the duties owed by one to the other; but Bushido held that the interest of the family and of the members thereof is intact—one and inseparable. This interest it bound up with affection—natural, instinctive, irresistible; hence, if we die for one we love with natural love (which animals themselves possess), what is that? "For if ye love them that love you, what reward have ye? Do not even the publicans the same?"

In his great history, Sanyo relates in touching language the heart struggle of Shigemori concerning his father's rebellious conduct. "If I be loyal, my father must be undone; if I obey my father, my duty to my sovereign must go amiss." Poor Shigemori! We see him afterward praying with all his soul that kind Heaven may visit him with death, that he may be released from this world where it is hard for purity and righteousness to dwell.

Many a Shigemori has his heart torn by the conflict between duty and affection. Indeed neither Shakespeare nor the Old Testament

itself contains an adequate rendering of *ko*, our conception of filial piety, and yet in such conflicts Bushido never wavered in its choice of Loyalty. Women, too, encouraged their offspring to sacrifice all for the king. Ever as resolute as Widow Windham and her illustrious consort, the samurai matron stood ready to give up her boys for the cause of Loyalty.

Since Bushido, like Aristotle and some modern sociologists, conceived the state as antedating the individual—the latter being born into the former as part and parcel thereof—he must live and die for it or for the incumbent of its legitimate authority. Readers of Crito will remember the argument with which Socrates represents the laws of the city as pleading with him on the subject of his escape. Among others he makes them (the laws, or the state) say: "Since you were begotten and nurtured and educated under us, dare you once to say you are not our offspring and servant, you and your fathers before you!" These are words which do not impress us as anything extraordinary; for the same thing has long been on the lips of Bushido, with this modification, that the laws and the state were represented with us by a personal being. Loyalty is an ethical outcome of this political theory.

I am not entirely ignorant of Mr. Spencer's view according to which political obedience—Loyalty—is accredited with only a transitional function.[18] It may be so. Sufficient unto the day is the virtue thereof. We may complacently repeat it, especially as we believe *that* day to be a long space of time, during which, so our national anthem says, "tiny pebbles grow into mighty rocks draped with moss." We may remember at this juncture that even among so democratic a people as the English, "the sentiment of personal fidelity to a man and his posterity which their Germanic ancestors felt for their chiefs, has," as Monsieur Boutmy recently said, "only passed more or less into their profound loyalty to the race and blood of their princes, as evidenced in their extraordinary attachment to the dynasty."

Political subordination, Mr. Spencer predicts, will give place to loyalty to the dictates of conscience. Suppose his induction is realized—will loyalty and its concomitant instinct of reverence

[18] *Principles of Ethics*, Vol. I, Pt. II, Ch. X.

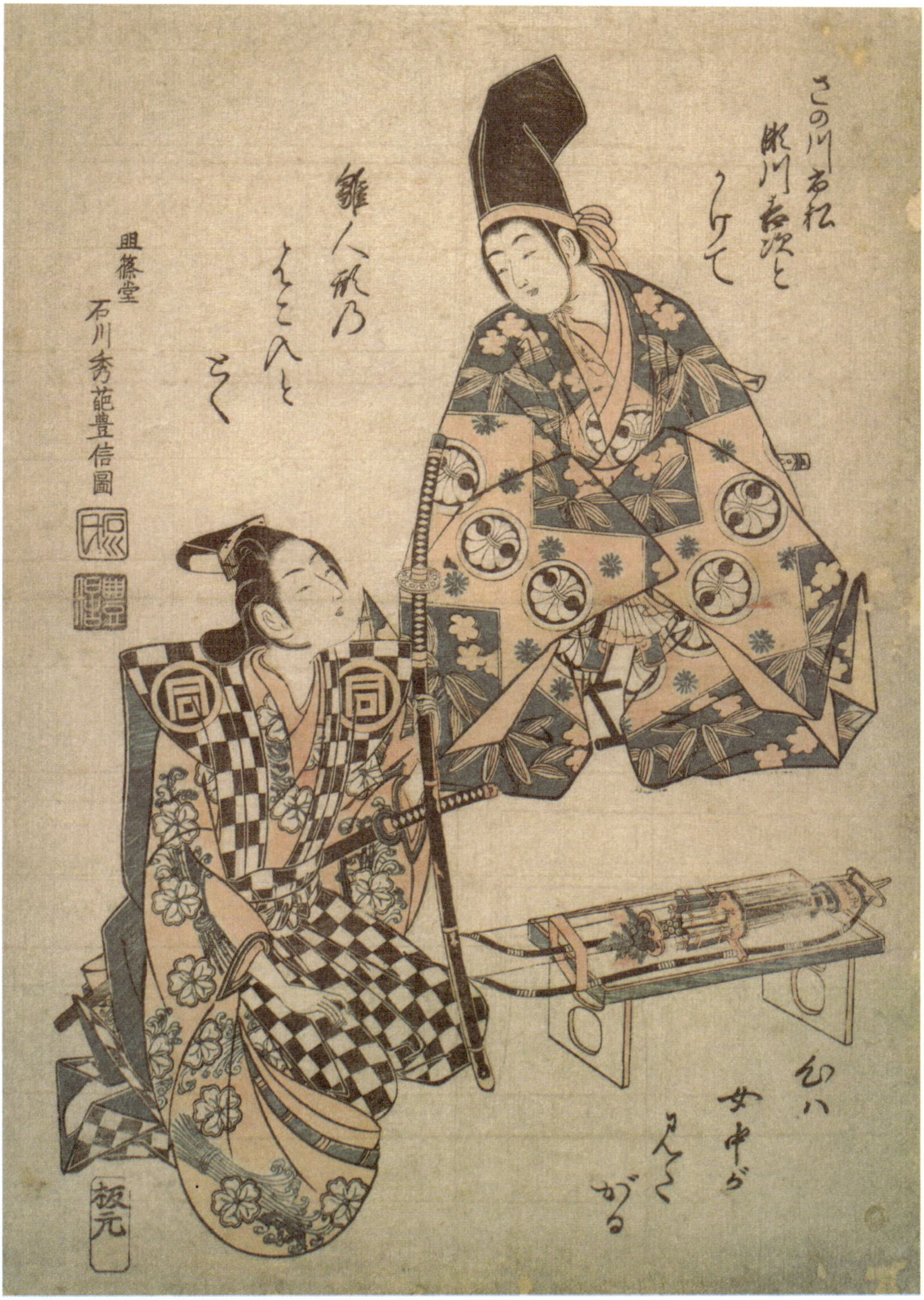

The actor Segawa Kichiji as a daimyō*'s young son, and Sanogawa Ichimatsu as a samurai attendant, woodblock print, circa 1750.*

disappear forever? We transfer our allegiance from one master to another, without being unfaithful to either; from being subjects of a ruler that wields the temporal sceptre we become servants of the monarch who sits enthroned in the penetralia of our heart. A few years ago a very stupid controversy, started by the misguided disciples of Spencer, made havoc among the reading class of Japan. In their zeal to uphold the claim of the throne to undivided loyalty, they charged Christians with treasonable propensities in that they avow fidelity to their Lord and Master. They arrayed forth sophistical arguments without the wit of Sophists, and scholastic tortuosities minus the niceties of the Schoolmen. Little did they know that we can, in a sense, "serve two masters without holding to the one or despising the other," "rendering unto Caesar the things that are Caesar's and unto God the things that are God's." Did not Socrates, all the while he unflinchingly refused to concede one iota of loyalty to his *daemon*, obey with equal fidelity and equanimity the command of his earthly master, the State? His conscience he followed, alive; his country he served, dying. Alack the day when a state grows so powerful as to demand of its citizens the dictates of their conscience!

Bushido did not require us to make our conscience the slave of any lord or king. Thomas Mowbray was a veritable spokesman for us when he said:

"Myself I throw, dread sovereign, at thy foot.
My life thou shalt command, but not my shame.
The one my duty owes; but my fair name,
Despite of death, that lives upon my grave,
To dark dishonor's use, thou shalt not have."

A man who sacrificed his own conscience to the capricious will or freak or fancy of a sovereign was accorded a low place in the estimate of the Precepts. Such an one was despised as *nei-shin*, a cringeling, who makes court by unscrupulous fawning or as *chô-shin*, a favorite who steals his master's affections by means of servile compliance; these two species of subjects corresponding exactly to those which Iago describes—the one, a duteous and knee-crooking knave, doting on his own obsequious bondage, wearing out his time much like his master's ass; the other trimm'd in forms and visages of duty, keeping yet his heart attending on himself. When a subject differed from his master, the loyal path for him to pursue was to use every available means to persuade him of his error, as Kent did to King Lear. Failing in this, let the master deal with him as he wills. In cases of this kind, it was quite a usual course for the samurai to make the last appeal to the intelligence and conscience of his lord by demonstrating the sincerity of his words with the shedding of his own blood.

Life being regarded as the means whereby to serve his master, and its ideal being set upon honor, the whole education and training of a samurai were conducted accordingly.

CHAPTER 10

武士の養成

Education and Training of a Samurai

The first point to observe in knightly pedagogics was to build up character, leaving in the shade the subtler faculties of prudence, intelligence and dialectics. We have seen the important part aesthetic accomplishments played in his education. Indispensable as they were to a man of culture, they were accessories rather than essentials of samurai training. Intellectual superiority was, of course, esteemed; but the word *Chi*, which was employed to denote intellectuality, meant wisdom in the first instance and placed knowledge only in a very subordinate place. The tripod that supported the framework of Bushido was said to be *Chi, Jin, Yu*, respectively Wisdom, Benevolence, and Courage. A samurai was essentially a man of action. Science was without the pale of his activity. He took advantage of it in so far as it concerned his profession of arms. Religion and theology were relegated to the priests; he concerned himself with them in so far as they helped to nourish courage. Like an English poet the samurai believed "'tis not the creed that saves the man; but it is the man that justifies the creed." Philosophy and literature formed the chief part of his intellectual training; but even in the pursuit of these, it was not objective truth that he strove after—literature was pursued mainly as a pastime, and philosophy as a practical aid in the formation of character, if not for the exposition of some military or political problem.

From what has been said, it will not be surprising to note that the curriculum of studies, according to the pedagogics of Bushido, consisted mainly of the following—fencing, archery, *jiujutsu* or *yawara*, horsemanship, the use of the spear, tactics, caligraphy, ethics,

A young samurai reading a scroll, watched by an older samurai who is listening (c. 1825), by Yashima Gakutei (1786–1868).

A samurai on horseback displays his archery skills for the Shogun (c 1897).

literature and history. Of these, *jiujutsu* and caligraphy may require a few words of explanation. Great stress was laid on good writing, probably because our logograms, partaking as they do of the nature of pictures, possess artistic value, and also because chirography was accepted as indicative of one's personal character. *Jiujutsu* may be briefly defined as an application of anatomical knowledge to the purpose of offense or defense. It differs from wrestling, in that it does not depend upon muscular strength. It differs from other forms of attack in that it uses no weapon. Its feat consists in clutching or striking such part of the enemy's body as will make him numb and incapable of resistance. Its object is not to kill, but to incapacitate one for action for the time being.

A subject of study which one would expect to find in military education and which is rather conspicuous by its absence in the Bushido course of instruction is mathematics. This, however, can be readily explained in part by the fact that feudal warfare was not carried on with scientific precision. Not only that, but the whole training of the samurai was unfavorable to fostering numerical notions.

Chivalry is uneconomical; it boasts of penury. It says with Ventidius that "ambition, the soldier's virtue, rather makes choice of loss, than gain which darkens him." Don Quixote takes more pride in his rusty spear and skin-and-bone horse than in gold and lands, and a samurai is in hearty sympathy with his exaggerated confrère of La Mancha. He disdains money itself, the art of making or hoarding it. It is to him veritably filthy lucre. The hackneyed expression to describe the decadence of an age is "that the civilians loved money and the soldiers feared death." Niggardliness of gold and of life excites as much disapprobation as their lavish use is panegyrized. "Less than all things," says a current precept, "men must grudge money: it is by riches that wisdom is hindered." Hence children were brought up with utter disregard of economy. It was considered bad taste to speak of it, and ignorance of the value of different coins was a token of good breeding. Knowledge of numbers was indispensable in the mustering of forces as well as in the distribution of benefices and fiefs; but the counting of money was left to meaner hands. In many feudatories, public finance was administered by a lower kind

A daimyō *(warlord) watches as trainees practice their sword skills with wooden* bokken.

of samurai or by priests. Every thinking *bushi* knew well enough that money formed the sinews of war; but he did not think of raising the appreciation of money to a virtue. It is true that thrift was enjoined by Bushido, but not for economical reasons so much as for the exercise of abstinence. Luxury was thought the greatest menace to manhood, and the severest simplicity was required of the warrior class, sumptuary laws being enforced in many of the clans.

We read that in ancient Rome the farmers of revenue and other financial agents were gradually raised to the rank of knights, the State thereby showing its appreciation of their service and of the importance of money itself. How closely this was connected with the luxury and avarice of the Romans may be imagined. Not so with the Precepts of Knighthood. These persisted in systematically regarding finance as something low—low as compared with moral and intellectual vocations.

Money and the love of it being thus diligently ignored, Bushido itself could long remain free from a thousand and one evils of which money is the root. This is sufficient reason for the fact that our public men have long been free from corruption; but, alas, how fast plutocracy is making its way in our time and generation!

The mental discipline which would now-a-days be chiefly aided by the study of mathematics, was supplied by literary exegesis and deontological discussions. Very few abstract subjects troubled the mind of the young, the chief aim of their education being, as I have said, decision of character. People whose minds were simply stored with information found no great admirers. Of the three services of studies that Bacon gives—for delight, ornament, and ability—Bushido had decided preference for the last, where their use was "in judgment and the disposition of business." Whether it was for the disposition of public business or for the exercise of self-control, it was with a practical end in view that education was conducted. "Learning without thought," said Confucius, "is labor lost: thought without learning is perilous."

When character and not intelligence, when the soul and not the head, is chosen by a teacher for the material to work upon and to

develop, his vocation partakes of a sacred character. "It is the parent who has borne me: it is the teacher who makes me man." With this idea, therefore, the esteem in which one's preceptor was held was very high. A man to evoke such confidence and respect from the young, must necessarily be endowed with superior personality without lacking erudition. He was a father to the fatherless, and an adviser to the erring. "Thy father and thy mother"—so runs our maxim—"are like heaven and earth; thy teacher and thy lord are like the sun and moon."

The present system of paying for every sort of service was not in vogue among the adherents of Bushido. It believed in a service which can be rendered only without money and without price. Spiritual service, be it of priest or teacher, was not to be repaid in gold or silver, not because it was valueless but because it was invaluable. Here the non-arithmetical honor-instinct of Bushido taught a truer lesson than modern Political Economy; for wages and salaries can be paid only for services whose results are definite, tangible, and measurable, whereas the best service done in education—namely, in soul development (and this includes the services of a pastor), is not definite, tangible or measurable. Being immeasurable, money, the ostensible measure of value, is of inadequate use. Usage sanctioned that pupils brought to their teachers money or goods at different seasons of the year; but these were not payments but offerings, which indeed were welcome to the recipients as they were usually men of stern calibre, boasting of honorable penury, too dignified to work with their hands and too proud to beg. They were grave personifications of high spirits undaunted by adversity. They were an embodiment of what was considered as an end of all learning, and were thus a living example of that discipline of disciplines, self-control.

A Japanese mother and child, by Yōshū Chikanobu (1838–1912), an influential woodblock print artist of the Meiji Period.

CHAPTER 11

自制心

Self-Control

The discipline of fortitude on the one hand, inculcating endurance without a groan, and the teaching of politeness on the other, requiring us not to mar the pleasure or serenity of another by manifestations of our own sorrow or pain, combined to engender a stoical turn of mind, and eventually to confirm it into a national trait of apparent stoicism. I say apparent stoicism, because I do not believe that true stoicism can ever become the characteristic of a whole nation, and also because some of our national manners and customs may seem to a foreign observer hard-hearted. Yet we are really as susceptible to tender emotion as any race under the sky.

I am inclined to think that in one sense we have to feel more than others—yes, doubly more—since the very attempt to, restrain natural promptings entails suffering. Imagine boys—and girls too—brought up not to resort to the shedding of a tear or the uttering of a groan for the relief of their feelings—and there is a physiological problem whether such effort steels their nerves or makes them more sensitive.

It was considered unmanly for a samurai to betray his emotions on his face. "He shows no sign of joy or anger," was a phrase used in describing a strong character. The most natural affections were kept under control. A father could embrace his son only at the expense of his dignity; a husband would not kiss his wife—no, not in the presence of other people, whatever he might do in private! There may be some truth in the remark of a witty youth when he said, "American husbands kiss their wives in public and beat them in private; Japanese husbands beat theirs in public and kiss them in private."

The great samurai Yatsuhashi, by Utagawa Kuniyoshi (1797–1861).

'Lovers Under Plum Blossoms', by Hokusai (1760–1849).

Calmness of behavior, composure of mind, should not be disturbed by passion of any kind. I remember when, during the late war with China, a regiment left a certain town, a large concourse of people flocked to the station to bid farewell to the general and his army. On this occasion an American resident resorted to the place, expecting to witness loud demonstrations, as the nation itself was highly excited and there were fathers, mothers, and sweethearts of the soldiers in the crowd. The American was strangely disappointed; for as the whistle blew and the train began to move, the hats of thousands of people were silently taken off and their heads bowed in reverential farewell; no waving of handkerchiefs, no word uttered, but deep silence in which only an attentive ear could catch a few broken sobs. In domestic life, too, I know of a father who spent whole nights listening to the breathing of a sick child, standing behind the door that he might not be caught in such an act of parental weakness! I know of a mother who, in her last moments, refrained from sending for her son, that he might not be disturbed in his studies. Our history and everyday life are replete with examples of heroic matrons who can well bear comparison with some of the most touching pages of Plutarch. Among our peasantry an Ian Maclaren would be sure to find many a Margaret Howe.

It is the same discipline of self-restraint which is accountable for the absence of more frequent revivals in the Christian churches of Japan. When a man or woman feels his or her soul stirred, the first instinct is to quietly suppress any indication of it. In rare instances is the tongue set free by an irresistible spirit, when we have eloquence of sincerity and fervor. It is putting a premium upon a breach of the third commandment to encourage speaking lightly of spiritual experience. It is truly jarring to Japanese ears to hear the most sacred words, the most secret heart experiences, thrown out in promiscuous audiences. "Dost thou feel the soil of thy soul stirred with tender thoughts? It is time for seeds to sprout. Disturb it not with speech; but let it work alone in quietness and secrecy," writes a young samurai in his diary.

To give in so many articulate words one's inmost thoughts and feelings—notably the religious—is taken among us as an unmistakable sign that they are neither very profound nor very

sincere. "Only a pomegranate is he"—so runs a popular saying—"who, when he gapes his mouth, displays the contents of his heart."

It is not altogether perverseness of oriental minds that the instant our emotions are moved we try to guard our lips in order to hide them. Speech is very often with us, as the Frenchman defined it, "the art of concealing thought."

Call upon a Japanese friend in time of deepest affliction and he will invariably receive you laughing, with red eyes or moist cheeks. At first you may think him hysterical. Press him for explanation and you will get a few broken commonplaces: "Human life has sorrow;" "They who meet must part;" "He that is born must die;" "It is foolish to count the years of a child that is gone, but a woman's heart will indulge in follies;" and the like. So the noble words of a noble Hohenzollern—"*Lerne zu leiden ohne Klagen*"—had found many responsive minds among us, long before they were uttered.

Indeed, the Japanese have recourse to risibility whenever the frailties of human nature are put to severest test. I think we possess a better reason than Democritus himself for our Abderian tendency; for laughter with us oftenest veils an effort to regain balance of temper, when disturbed by any untoward circumstance. It is a counterpoise of sorrow or rage.

The suppression of feelings being thus steadily insisted upon, they find their safety-valve in poetical aphorism. A poet of the tenth century writes, "In Japan and China as well, humanity, when moved by sorrow, tells its bitter grief in verse." A mother who tries to console her broken heart by fancying her departed child absent on his wonted chase after the dragon-fly, hums,

"How far to-day in chase, I wonder,
Has gone my hunter of the dragon-fly!"

I refrain from quoting other examples, for I know I could do only scant justice to the pearly gems of our literature, were I to render into a foreign tongue the thoughts which were wrung drop by drop from bleeding hearts and threaded into beads of rarest value. I hope I have in a measure shown that inner working of our minds which often presents an appearance of callousness or of an hysterical mixture of laughter and dejection, and whose sanity is sometimes called in question.

It has also been suggested that our endurance of pain and indifference to death are due to less sensitive nerves. This is plausible as far as it goes. The next question is: Why are our nerves less tightly strung? It may be our climate is not so stimulating as the American. It may be our monarchical form of government does not excite us as much as the Republic does the Frenchman. It may be that we do not read *Sartor Resartus*[19] as zealously as the Englishman. Personally, I believe it was our very excitability and sensitiveness which made it a necessity to recognize and enforce constant self-repression; but whatever may be the explanation, without taking into account long years of discipline in self-control, none can be correct.

Discipline in self-control can easily go too far. It can well repress the genial current of the soul. It can force pliant natures into distortions and monstrosities. It can beget bigotry, breed hypocrisy or hebetate affections. Be a virtue never so noble, it has its counterpart and counterfeit. We must recognize in each virtue its own positive excellence and follow its positive ideal, and the ideal of self-restraint is to keep our mind *level*—as our expression is—or, to borrow a Greek term, attain the state of *euthymia,* which Democritus called the highest good.

The acme of self-control is reached and best illustrated in the first of the two institutions which we shall now bring to view; namely, the institutions of suicide and redress.

[19] An 1836 novel by Thomas Carlyle.

CHAPTER 12

切腹と敵討ち

The Institutions of Suicide and Redress

Of these two institutions (the former known as *hara-kiri* and the latter as *kataki-uchi*), many foreign writers have treated more or less fully.

To begin with suicide, let me state that I confine my observations only to *seppuku* or *kappuku*, popularly known as *hara-kiri*—which means self-immolation by disembowelment. "Ripping the abdomen? How absurd!"—so cry those to whom the name is new. Absurdly odd as it may sound at first to foreign ears, it can not be so very foreign to students of Shakespeare, who puts these words in Brutus' mouth—"Thy (Caesar's) spirit walks abroad and turns our swords into our proper entrails." Listen to a modern English poet, who in his *Light of Asia*, speaks of a sword piercing the bowels of a queen: none blames him for bad English or breach of modesty. Or, to take still another example, look at Guercino's painting of Cato's death, in the Palazzo Rossa in Genoa. Whoever has read the swan-song which Addison makes Cato sing, will not jeer at the sword half-buried in his abdomen. In our minds this mode of death is associated with instances of noblest deeds and of most touching pathos, so that nothing repugnant, much less ludicrous, mars our conception of it. So wonderful is the transforming power of virtue, of greatness, of tenderness, that the vilest form of death assumes a sublimity and becomes a symbol of new life, or else—the sign which Constantine beheld would not conquer the world!

Not for extraneous associations only does *seppuku* lose in our mind any taint of absurdity; for the choice of this particular part of

An old samurai contemplates seppuku *(ritual suicide).*

the body to operate upon, was based on an old anatomical belief as to the seat of the soul and of the affections. When Moses wrote of Joseph's "bowels yearning upon his brother," or David prayed the Lord not to forget his bowels, or when Isaiah, Jeremiah and other inspired men of old spoke of the "sounding" or the "troubling" of bowels, they all and each endorsed the belief prevalent among the Japanese that in the abdomen was enshrined the soul. The Semites habitually spoke of the liver and kidneys and surrounding fat as the seat of emotion and of life. The term *hara* was more comprehensive than the Greek *phren* or *thumos* and the Japanese and Hellenese alike thought the spirit of man to dwell somewhere in that region. Such a notion is by no means confined to the peoples of antiquity. The French, in spite of the theory propounded by one of their most distinguished philosophers, Descartes, that the soul is located in the pineal gland, still insist in using the term *ventre* in a sense, which, if anatomically too vague, is nevertheless physiologically significant. Similarly *entrailles* stands in their language for affection and compassion. Nor is such belief mere superstition, being more scientific than the general idea of making the heart the center of the feelings. Without asking a friar, the Japanese knew better than Romeo "in what vile part of this anatomy one's name did lodge." Modern neurologists speak of the abdominal and pelvic brains, denoting thereby sympathetic nerve-centers in those parts which are strongly affected by any psychical action. This view of mental physiology once admitted, the syllogism of *seppuku* is easy to construct. "I will open the seat of my soul and show you how it fares with it. See for yourself whether it is polluted or clean."

I do not wish to be understood as asserting religious or even moral justification of suicide, but the high estimate placed upon honor was ample excuse with many for taking one's own life. How many acquiesced in the sentiment expressed by Garth,

> "When honor's lost, 'tis a relief to die;
> Death's but a sure retreat from infamy,"

and have smilingly surrendered their souls to oblivion! Death when honor was involved, was accepted in Bushido as a key to the solution of many complex problems, so that to an ambitious samurai a natural departure from life seemed a rather tame affair and a consummation not devoutly to be wished for. I dare say that many good Christians, if only they are honest enough, will confess the fascination of, if not positive admiration for, the sublime composure with which Cato, Brutus, Petronius and a host of other ancient worthies, terminated their own earthly existence. Is it too bold to hint that the death of the first of the philosophers was partly suicidal? When we are told so minutely by his pupils how their master willingly submitted to the mandate of the state—which he knew was morally mistaken—in spite of the possibilities of escape, and how he took up the cup of hemlock in his own hand, even offering libation from its deadly contents, do we not discern in his whole proceeding and demeanor, an act of self-immolation? No physical compulsion here, as in ordinary cases of execution. True the verdict of the judges was compulsory: it said, "Thou shalt die, and that by thy own hand." If suicide meant no more than dying by one's own hand, Socrates was a clear case of suicide. But nobody would charge him with the crime; Plato, who was averse to it, would not call his master a suicide.

Now my readers will understand that *seppuku* was not a mere suicidal process. It was an institution, legal and ceremonial. An invention of the middle ages, it was a process by which warriors could expiate their crimes, apologize for errors, escape from disgrace, redeem their friends, or prove their sincerity. When enforced as a legal punishment, it was practiced with due ceremony. It was a refinement of self-destruction, and none could perform it without the utmost coolness of temper and composure of demeanor, and for these reasons it was particularly befitting the profession of *bushi*.

Antiquarian curiosity, if nothing else, would tempt me to give here a description of this obsolete ceremonial; but seeing that such a description was made by a far abler writer, whose book is not much read now-a-days, I am tempted to make a somewhat lengthy quotation. Mitford, in his *Tales of Old Japan*, after giving a translation of a treatise on *seppuku* from a rare Japanese manuscript, goes on to describe an instance of such an execution of which he was an eye-witness:

"We (seven foreign representatives) were invited to follow the Japanese witness into the *hondo* or main hall of the temple, where the

A seppuku *(ritual suicide) ceremony performed in front of a lord.*

ceremony was to be performed. It was an imposing scene. A large hall with a high roof supported by dark pillars of wood. From the ceiling hung a profusion of those huge gilt lamps and ornaments peculiar to Buddhist temples. In front of the high altar, where the floor, covered with beautiful white mats, is raised some three or four inches from the ground, was laid a rug of scarlet felt. Tall candles placed at regular intervals gave out a dim mysterious light, just sufficient to let all the proceedings be seen. The seven Japanese took their places on the left of the raised floor, the seven foreigners on the right. No other person was present.

"After the interval of a few minutes of anxious suspense, Taki Zenzaburo, a stalwart man thirty-two years of age, with a noble air, walked into the hall attired in his dress of ceremony, with the peculiar hempen-cloth wings which are worn on great occasions. He was accompanied by a *kaishaku* and three officers, who wore the *jimbaori* or war surcoat with gold tissue facings. The word *kaishaku* it should be observed, is one to which our word executioner is no equivalent term. The office is that of a gentleman: in many cases it is performed by a kinsman or friend of the condemned, and the relation between them is rather that of principal and second than that of victim and executioner. In this instance the *kaishaku* was a pupil of Taki Zenzaburo, and was selected by friends of the latter from among their own number for his skill in swordsmanship.

"With the *kaishaku* on his left hand, Taki Zenzaburo advanced slowly towards the Japanese witnesses, and the two bowed before them, then drawing near to the foreigners they saluted us in the same way, perhaps even with more deference; in each case the salutation was ceremoniously returned. Slowly and with great dignity the condemned man mounted on to the raised floor, prostrated himself before the high altar twice, and seated himself[20] on the felt carpet with his back to the high altar, the *kaishaku* crouching on his left hand side. One of the three attendant officers then came forward, bearing a stand of the kind used in the temple for offerings, on which, wrapped in paper, lay the *wakizashi*, the short sword or dirk of the Japanese, nine inches and a half in length, with a point and

[20] Seated himself—that is, in the Japanese fashion, his knees and toes touching the ground and his body resting on his heels. In this position, which is one of respect, he remained until his death.

an edge as sharp as a razor's. This he handed, prostrating himself, to the condemned man, who received it reverently, raising it to his head with both hands, and placed it in front of himself.

"After another profound obeisance, Taki Zenzaburo, in a voice which betrayed just so much emotion and hesitation as might be expected from a man who is making a painful confession, but with no sign of either in his face or manner, spoke as follows:

> 'I, and I alone, unwarrantably gave the order to fire on the foreigners at Kobe, and again as they tried to escape. For this crime I disembowel myself, and I beg you who are present to do me the honor of witnessing the act.'

"Bowing once more, the speaker allowed his upper garments to slip down to his girdle, and remained naked to the waist. Carefully, according to custom, he tucked his sleeves under his knees to prevent himself from falling backward; for a noble Japanese gentleman should die falling forwards. Deliberately, with a steady hand he took the dirk that lay before him; he looked at it wistfully, almost affectionately; for a moment he seemed to collect his thoughts for the last time, and then stabbing himself deeply below the waist in the left-hand side, he drew the dirk slowly across to his right side, and turning it in the wound, gave a slight cut upwards. During this sickeningly painful operation he never moved a muscle of his face. When he drew out the dirk, he leaned forward and stretched out his neck; an expression of pain for the first time crossed his face, but he uttered no sound. At that moment the *kaishaku*, who, still crouching by his side, had been keenly watching his every movement, sprang to his feet, poised his sword for a second in the air; there was a flash, a heavy, ugly thud, a crashing fall; with one blow the head had been severed from the body.

"A dead silence followed, broken only by the hideous noise of the blood throbbing out of the inert head before us, which but a moment before had been a brave and chivalrous man. It was horrible.

"The *kaishaku* made a low bow, wiped his sword with a piece of paper which he had ready for the purpose, and retired from the

The ritual suicide of Taki Zenzaburo.

Tokugawa Ieyasu (1543–1616) was the founder and first shōgun *of the Tokugawa shogunate, which ruled Japan from 1603 until the Meiji Restoration in 1868.*

raised floor; and the stained dirk was solemnly borne away, a bloody proof of the execution.

"The two representatives of the Mikado then left their places, and crossing over to where the foreign witnesses sat, called to us to witness that the sentence of death upon Taki Zenzaburo had been faithfully carried out. The ceremony being at an end, we left the temple."

I might multiply any number of descriptions of *seppuku* from literature or from the relation of eye-witnesses; but one more instance will suffice.

Two brothers, Sakon and Naiki, respectively twenty-four and seventeen years of age, made an effort to kill Iyéyasu in order to avenge their father's wrongs; but before they could enter the camp they were made prisoners. The old general admired the pluck of the youths who dared an attempt on his life and ordered that they should be allowed to die an honorable death. Their little brother Hachimaro, a mere infant of eight summers, was condemned to a similar fate, as the sentence was pronounced on all the male members of the family, and the three were taken to a monastery where it was to be executed. A physician who was present on the occasion has left us a diary from which the following scene is translated. "When they were all seated in a row for final despatch, Sakon turned to the youngest and said—'Go thou first, for I wish to be sure that thou doest it aright.' Upon the little one's replying that, as he had never seen *seppuku* performed, he would like to see his brothers do it and then he could follow them, the older brothers smiled between their tears: 'Well said, little fellow! So canst thou well boast of being our father's child.' When they had placed him between them, Sakon thrust the dagger into the left side of his own abdomen and asked: 'Look, brother! Dost understand now? Only, don't push the dagger too far, lest thou fall back. Lean forward, rather, and keep thy knees well composed.' Naiki did likewise and said to the boy: 'Keep thy eyes open or else thou mayst look like a dying woman. If thy dagger feels anything within and thy strength fails, take courage and double thy effort to cut across.' The child looked from one to the other, and when both had expired, he calmly half denuded himself and followed the example set him on either hand."

Royal envoys deliver the message that Enya Hangan (Asano Naganori) is to committ seppuku. *The third man (right) is possibly Hangan brandishing a dagger with which to disembowl himself.*

The glorification of *seppuku* offered, naturally enough, no small temptation to its unwarranted committal. For causes entirely incompatible with reason, or for reasons entirely undeserving of death, hot-headed youths rushed into it as insects fly into fire; mixed and dubious motives drove more samurai to this deed than nuns into convent gates. Life was cheap—cheap as reckoned by the popular standard of honor. The saddest feature was that honor, which was always in the *agio*, so to speak, was not always solid gold, but alloyed with baser metals. No one circle in the Inferno will boast of greater density of Japanese population than the seventh, to which Dante consigns all victims of self-destruction!

And yet, for a true samurai to hasten death or to court it, was alike cowardice. A typical fighter, when he lost battle after battle and was pursued from plain to hill and from bush to cavern, found himself hungry and alone in the dark hollow of a tree, his sword blunt with use, his bow broken and arrows exhausted—did not the noblest of the Romans fall upon his own sword in Phillippi under like circumstances? Deemed it cowardly to die, but with a fortitude approaching a Christian martyr's, cheered himself with an impromptu verse:

"Come! evermore come,
Ye dread sorrows and pains!
And heap on my burden'd back;
That I not one test may lack
Of what strength in me remains!"

This, then, was the Bushido teaching—Bear and face all calamities and adversities with patience and a pure conscience; for as Mencius[21] taught, "When Heaven is about to confer a great office on anyone, it first exercises his mind with suffering and his sinews and bones with toil; it exposes his body to hunger and subjects him to extreme poverty; and it confounds his undertakings. In all these ways it stimulates his mind, hardens his nature, and supplies his incompetencies." True honor lies in fulfilling Heaven's decree and no death incurred in so doing is ignominious, whereas death to avoid what Heaven has in store is cowardly indeed! In that quaint book

[21] I use Dr. Legge's translation verbatim.

of Sir Thomas Browne's, *Religio Medici,* there is an exact English equivalent for what is repeatedly taught in our Precepts. Let me quote it: "It is a brave act of valor to contemn death, but where life is more terrible than death, it is then the truest valor to dare to live." A renowned priest of the seventeenth century satirically observed: "Talk as he may, a samurai who ne'er has died is apt in decisive moments to flee or hide." Again—Him who once has died in the bottom of his breast, no spears of Sanada nor all the arrows of Tametomo can pierce. How near we come to the portals of the temple whose Builder taught, "he that loseth his life for my sake shall find it!" These are but a few of the numerous examples which tend to confirm the moral identity of the human species, notwithstanding an attempt so assiduously made to render the distinction between Christian and Pagan as great as possible.

We have thus seen that the Bushido institution of suicide was neither so irrational nor barbarous as its abuse strikes us at first sight. We will now see whether its sister institution of Redress—or call it Revenge, if you will—has its mitigating features. I hope I can dispose of this question in a few words, since a similar institution, or call it custom, if that suits you better, has at some time prevailed among all peoples and has not yet become entirely obsolete, as attested by the continuance of duelling and lynching. Why, has not an American captain recently challenged Esterhazy, that the wrongs of Dreyfus be avenged? Among a savage tribe which has no marriage, adultery is not a sin, and only the jealousy of a lover protects a woman from abuse: so in a time which has no criminal court, murder is not a crime, and only the vigilant vengeance of the victim's people preserves social order. "What is the most beautiful thing on earth?" said Osiris to Horus. The reply was, "To avenge a parent's wrongs"—to which a Japanese would have added "and a master's."

In revenge there is something which satisfies one's sense of justice. The avenger reasons: "My good father did not deserve death. He who killed him did great evil. My father, if he were alive, would not tolerate a deed like this: Heaven itself hates wrong-doing. It is the will of my father; it is the will of Heaven that the evil-doer cease from his work. He must perish by my hand; because he shed my father's blood, I, who am his flesh and blood, must shed the murderer's. The

From a nineteenth century series of woodcut prints entitled, 'Loyalty, Filial Piety and Revenge'.

same Heaven shall not shelter him and me." The ratiocination is simple and childish (though we know Hamlet did not reason much more deeply), nevertheless it shows an innate sense of exact balance and equal justice "An eye for an eye, a tooth for a tooth." Our sense of revenge is as exact as our mathematical faculty, and until both terms of the equation are satisfied we cannot get over the sense of something left undone.

In Judaism, which believed in a jealous God, or in Greek mythology, which provided a Nemesis, vengeance may be left to superhuman agencies; but common sense furnished Bushido with the institution of redress as a kind of ethical court of equity, where people could take cases not to be judged in accordance with ordinary law. The master of the forty-seven Ronins was condemned to death—he had no court of higher instance to appeal to; his faithful retainers addressed themselves to Vengeance, the only Supreme Court existing; they in their turn were condemned by common law—but the popular instinct passed a different judgment and hence their memory is still kept as green and fragrant as are their graves at Sengakuji to this day.

Though Lao-Tse taught to recompense injury with kindness, the voice of Confucius was very much louder, which counselled that injury must be recompensed with justice—and yet revenge was justified only when it was undertaken in behalf of our superiors and benefactors. One's own wrongs, including injuries done to wife and children, were to be borne and forgiven. A samurai could therefore fully sympathize with Hannibal's oath to avenge his country's wrongs, but he scorns James Hamilton for wearing in his girdle a handful of earth from his wife's grave, as an eternal incentive to avenge her wrongs on the Regent Murray.

Both of these institutions of suicide and redress lost their *raison d'être* at the promulgation of the criminal code. No more do we hear of romantic adventures of a fair maiden as she tracks in disguise the murderer of her parent. No more can we witness tragedies of family vendetta enacted. The knight errantry of Miyamoto Musashi is now a tale of the past. The well-ordered police spies out the criminal for the injured party and the law metes out justice. The whole state and society will see that wrong is righted. The sense of justice satisfied, there is no need of *kataki-uchi*. If this had meant that "hunger of the heart which feeds upon the hope of glutting that hunger with the life-blood of the victim," as a New England divine has described it, a few paragraphs in the Criminal Code would not so entirely have made an end of it.

As to *seppuku*, though it too has no existence *de jure*, we still hear of it from time to time, and shall continue to hear, I am afraid, as long as the past is remembered. Many painless and time-saving methods of self-immolation will come in vogue, as its votaries are increasing with fearful rapidity throughout the world; but Professor Morselli will have to concede to *seppuku* an aristocratic position among them. He maintains that "when suicide is accomplished by very painful means or at the cost of prolonged agony, in ninety-nine cases out of a hundred, it may be assigned as the act of a mind disordered by fanaticism, by madness, or by morbid excitement."[22] But a normal *seppuku* does not savor of fanaticism, or madness or excitement, utmost *sang froid* being necessary to its successful accomplishment. Of the two kinds into which Dr. Strahan[23] divides suicide, the Rational or Quasi, and the Irrational or True, *seppuku* is the best example of the former type.

From these bloody institutions, as well as from the general tenor of Bushido, it is easy to infer that the sword played an important part in social discipline and life. The saying passed as an axiom, which called the sword the soul of the samurai.

[22] Morselli, *Suicide*, p. 314.

[23] *Suicide and Insanity*, 1893.

CHAPTER 13

武士の刀、魂

The Sword, the Soul of the Samurai

The sword was made the emblem of power and prowess. When Mahomet proclaimed that "The sword is the key of Heaven and of Hell," he only echoed a Japanese sentiment. Very early the samurai boy learned to wield it. It was a momentous occasion for him when at the age of five he was apparelled in the paraphernalia of samurai costume, placed upon a *go*-board[24] and initiated into the rights of the military profession by having thrust into his girdle a real sword, instead of the toy dirk with which he had been playing. After this first ceremony of *adoptio per arma*, he was no more to be seen outside his father's gates without this badge of his status, even if it was usually substituted for everyday wear by a gilded wooden dirk. Not many years pass before he wears constantly the genuine steel, though blunt, and then the sham arms are thrown aside and with enjoyment keener than his newly acquired blades, he marches out to try their edge on wood and stone. When be reaches man's estate at the age of fifteen, being given independence of action, he can now pride himself upon the possession of arms sharp enough for any work. The very possession of the dangerous instrument imparts to him a feeling and an air of self-respect and responsibility. "He beareth not his sword in vain." What he carries in his belt is a symbol of what he carries in his mind and heart—Loyalty and Honor. The two swords, the longer and the shorter—called respectively *daito* and *shoto* or *katana* and *wakizashi*—never leave his side. When at home, they grace the most conspicuous place in study or parlor; by night they guard his pillow within easy reach of his hand. Constant companions, they are beloved, and proper

[24] The game of *go* is sometimes called Japanese checkers, but is much more intricate than the English game. The *go*-board contains 361 squares and is supposed to represent a battlefield—the object of the game being to occupy as much space as possible.

A woman accompanies two boys playing at a daimyō *procession. At the front, a boy holds a broom in his right hand as a spear and between his belt a dustpan as a sword, while he is followed by a boy on a hobby horse. From an eighteenth century woodcut by Suzuki Harunobu.*

'The Swordsmith' (1802), by Katsushika Hokusai.

names of endearment given them. Being venerated, they are well-nigh worshiped. The Father of History has recorded as a curious piece of information that the Scythians sacrificed to an iron scimitar. Many a temple and many a family in Japan hoards a sword as an object of adoration. Even the commonest dirk has due respect paid to it. Any insult to it is tantamount to personal affront. Woe to him who carelessly steps over a weapon lying on the floor!

So precious an object cannot long escape the notice and the skill of artists nor the vanity of its owner, especially in times of peace, when it is worn with no more use than a crosier by a bishop or a sceptre by a king. Shark-skin and finest silk for hilt, silver and gold for guard, lacquer of varied hues for scabbard, robbed the deadliest weapon of half its terror; but these appurtenances are playthings compared with the blade itself.

The swordsmith was not a mere artisan but an inspired artist and his workshop a sanctuary. Daily he commenced his craft with prayer and purification, or, as the phrase was, "he committed his soul and spirit into the forging and tempering of the steel." Every swing of the sledge, every plunge into water, every friction on the grindstone, was a religious act of no slight import. Was it the spirit of the master or of his tutelary god that cast a formidable spell over our sword? Perfect as a work of art, setting at defiance its Toledo and Damascus rivals, there is more than art could impart. Its cold blade, collecting on its surface the moment it is drawn the vapors of the atmosphere; its immaculate texture, flashing light of bluish hue; its matchless edge, upon which histories and possibilities hang; the curve of its back, uniting exquisite grace with utmost strength—all these thrill us with mixed feelings of power and beauty, of awe and terror. Harmless were its mission, if it only remained a thing of beauty and joy! But, ever within reach of the hand, it presented no small temptation for abuse. Too often did the blade flash forth from its peaceful sheath. The abuse sometimes went so far as to try the acquired steel on some harmless creature's neck.

The question that concerns us most is, however, Did Bushido justify the promiscuous use of the weapon? The answer is unequivocally, no! As it laid great stress on its proper use, so did it

'The Fourth Matsumoto Koshiro as a Samurai' (1782), by Katsukawa Shunshō.

denounce and abhor its misuse. A dastard or a braggart was he who brandished his weapon on undeserved occasions. A self-possessed man knows the right time to use it, and such times come but rarely. Let us listen to the late Count Katsu, who passed through one of the most turbulent times of our history, when assassinations, suicides, and other sanguinary practices were the order of the day. Endowed as he once was with almost dictatorial powers, repeatedly marked out as an object for assassination, he never tarnished his sword with blood. In relating some of his reminiscences to a friend he says, in a quaint, plebeian way peculiar to him: "I have a great dislike for killing people and so I haven't killed one single man. I have released those whose heads should have been chopped off. A friend said to me one day, 'You don't kill enough. Don't you eat pepper and egg-plants?' Well, some people are no better! But you see that fellow was slain himself. My escape may be due to my dislike of killing. I had the hilt of my sword so tightly fastened to the scabbard that it was hard to draw the blade. I made up my mind that though they cut me, I will not cut. Yes, yes! some people are truly like fleas and mosquitoes and they bite—but what does their biting amount to? It itches a little, that's all; it won't endanger life." These are the words of one whose Bushido training was tried in the fiery furnace of adversity and triumph. The popular apothegm—"To be beaten is to conquer," meaning true conquest consists in not opposing a riotous foe; and "The best won victory is that obtained without shedding of blood," and others of similar import—will show that after all the ultimate ideal of knighthood was Peace.

It was a great pity that this high ideal was left exclusively to priests and moralists to preach, while the samurai went on practicing and extolling martial traits. In this they went so far as to tinge the ideals of womanhood with Amazonian character. Here we may profitably devote a few paragraphs to the subject of the training and position of woman.

CHAPTER 14

武家の女性の在り方

The Training and Position of Woman

The female half of our species has sometimes been called the paragon of paradoxes, because the intuitive working of its mind is beyond the comprehension of men's "arithmetical understanding." The Chinese ideogram denoting "the mysterious," "the unknowable," consists of two parts, one meaning "young" and the other "woman," because the physical charms and delicate thoughts of the fair sex are above the coarse mental calibre of our sex to explain.

In the Bushido ideal of woman, however, there is little mystery and only a seeming paradox. I have said that it was Amazonian, but that is only half the truth. Ideographically the Chinese represent wife by a woman holding a broom—certainly not to brandish it offensively or defensively against her conjugal ally, neither for witchcraft, but for the more harmless uses for which the besom was first invented—the idea involved being thus not less homely than the etymological derivation of the English wife (weaver) and daughter (*duhitar,* milk maid). Without confining the sphere of woman's activity to *Küche, Kirche, Kinder,* as the present German Kaiser is said to do, the Bushido ideal of womanhood was preeminently domestic. These seeming contradictions—Domesticity and Amazonian traits—are not inconsistent with the Precepts of Knighthood, as we shall see.

Bushido being a teaching primarily intended for the masculine sex, the virtues it prized in woman were naturally far from being distinctly feminine. Winckelmann remarks that "the supreme beauty of Greek art is rather male than female," and Lecky adds that it was

This 1802 print shows the wife of a samurai reading books, with another woman writing with a pen, one looking at ukiyo-e *prints, one folding paper and another delivering reams of paper and ink.*

The female warrior Hangaku, woodblock print (1885).

true in the moral conception of the Greeks as in their art. Bushido similarly praised those women most "who emancipated themselves from the frailty of their sex and displayed an heroic fortitude worthy of the strongest and the bravest of men."[25] Young girls therefore, were trained to repress their feelings, to indurate their nerves, to manipulate weapons—especially the long-handled sword called *nagi-nata*, so as to be able to hold their own against unexpected odds. Yet the primary motive for exercises of this martial character was not for use in the field; it was twofold—personal and domestic. Woman owning no suzerain of her own, formed her own bodyguard. With her weapon she guarded her personal sanctity with as much zeal as her husband did his master's. The domestic utility of her warlike training was in the education of her sons, as we shall see later.

Fencing and similar exercises, if rarely of practical use, were a wholesome counterbalance to the otherwise sedentary habits of woman. But these exercises were not followed only for hygienic purposes. They could be turned into use in times of need. Girls, when they reached womanhood, were presented with dirks (*kai-ken*, pocket poniards), which might be directed to the bosom of their assailants, or, if advisable, to their own. The latter was very often the case: and yet I will not judge them severely. Even the Christian conscience with its horror of self-immolation, will not be harsh with them, seeing Pelagia and Domnina, two suicides, were canonized for their purity and piety. When a Japanese Virginia saw her chastity menaced, she did not wait for her father's dagger. Her own weapon lay always in her bosom. It was a disgrace to her not to know the proper way in which she had to perpetrate self-destruction. For example, little as she was taught in anatomy, she must know the exact spot to cut in her throat: she must know how to tie her lower limbs together with a belt so that, whatever the agonies of death might be, her corpse be found in utmost modesty with the limbs properly composed. Is not a caution like this worthy of the Christian Perpetua or the Vestal Cornelia? I would not put such an abrupt interrogation, were it not for a misconception, based on our bathing customs and other trifles, that chastity is unknown among us.[26] On the contrary, chastity was a pre-eminent virtue of the samurai woman, held above

[25] Lecky, *History of European Morals II*, p. 383.
[26] For a very sensible explanation of nudity and bathing see Finck's *Lotos Time in Japan*, pp. 286–297.

life itself. A young woman, taken prisoner, seeing herself in danger of violence at the hands of the rough soldiery, says she will obey their pleasure, provided she be first allowed to write a line to her sisters, whom war has dispersed in every direction. When the epistle is finished, off she runs to the nearest well and saves her honor by drowning. The letter she leaves behind ends with these verses:

> "For fear lest clouds may dim her light,
> Should she but graze this nether sphere,
> The young moon poised above the height
> Doth hastily betake to flight."

It would be unfair to give my readers an idea that masculinity alone was our highest ideal for woman. Far from it! Accomplishments and the gentler graces of life were required of them. Music, dancing and literature were not neglected. Some of the finest verses in our literature were expressions of feminine sentiments; in fact, women played an important role in the history of Japanese *belles lettres.* Dancing was taught (I am speaking of samurai girls and not of *geisha*) only to smooth the angularity of their movements. Music was to regale the weary hours of their fathers and husbands; hence it was not for the technique, the art as such, that music was learned; for the ultimate object was purification of heart, since it was said that no harmony of sound is attainable without the player's heart being in harmony with herself. Here again we see the same idea prevailing which we notice in the training of youths—that accomplishments were ever kept subservient to moral worth. Just enough of music and dancing to add grace and brightness to life, but never to foster vanity and extravagance. I sympathize with the Persian prince, who, when taken into a ball-room in London and asked to take part in the merriment, bluntly remarked that in his country they provided a particular set of girls to do that kind of business for them.

The accomplishments of our women were not acquired for show or social ascendency. They were a home diversion; and if they shone in social parties, it was as the attributes of a hostess—in other words, as a part of the household contrivance for hospitality. Domesticity guided their education. It may be said that the accomplishments of the women of Old Japan, be they martial or pacific in character,

A music teacher of the Kaei era (1848–1854) smiles as she plays her shamisen. *From the series* Fuzoku sanjuniso, *'Thirty-Two Aspects of Customs and Manners.'*

'The Marriage Ceremony' (c. 1768), by Suzuki Harunobu. This print shows the ironaoshi *ceremony in which the bride is helped by attendants to change from her white silk wedding robes into ordinary clothes.*

were mainly intended for the home; and, however far they might roam, they never lost sight of the hearth as the center. It was to maintain its honor and integrity that they slaved, drudged and gave up their lives. Night and day, in tones at once firm and tender, brave and plaintive, they sang to their little nests. As daughter, woman sacrificed herself for her father, as wife for her husband, and as mother for her son. Thus from earliest youth she was taught to deny herself. Her life was not one of independence, but of dependent service. Man's helpmeet, if her presence is helpful she stays on the stage with him: if it hinders his work, she retires behind the curtain. Not infrequently does it happen that a youth becomes enamored of a maiden who returns his love with equal ardor, but, when she realizes his interest in her makes him forgetful of his duties, disfigures her person that her attractions may cease. Adzuma, the ideal wife in the minds of samurai girls, finds herself loved by a man who, in order to win her affection, conspires against her husband. Upon pretence of joining in the guilty plot, she manages in the dark to take her husband's place, and the sword of the lover assassin descends upon her own devoted head.

The following epistle written by the wife of a young *daimio*, before taking her own life, needs no comment: "Oft have I heard that no accident or chance ever mars the march of events here below, and that all moves in accordance with a plan. To take shelter under a common bough or a drink of the same river, is alike ordained from ages prior to our birth. Since we were joined in ties of eternal wedlock, now two short years ago, my heart hath followed thee, even as its shadow followeth an object, inseparably bound heart to heart, loving and being loved. Learning but recently, however, that the coming battle is to be the last of thy labor and life, take the farewell greeting of thy loving partner. I have heard that Kō-u, the mighty warrior of ancient China, lost a battle, loth to part with his favorite Gu. Yoshinaka, too, brave as he was, brought disaster to his cause, too weak to bid prompt farewell to his wife. Why should I, to whom earth no longer offers hope or joy—why should I detain thee or thy thoughts by living? Why should I not, rather, await thee on the road which all mortal kind must sometime tread? Never, prithee, never forget the many benefits which our good master Hideyori hath heaped upon thee. The gratitude we owe him is as deep as the sea and as high as the hills."

Woman's surrender of herself to the good of her husband, home and family, was as willing and honorable as the man's self-surrender to the good of his lord and country. Self-renunciation, without which no life-enigma can be solved, was the keynote of the Loyalty of man as well as of the Domesticity of woman. She was no more the slave of man than was her husband of his liege-lord, and the part she played was recognized as *Naijo*, "the inner help." In the ascending scale of service stood woman, who annihilated herself for man, that he might annihilate himself for the master, that he in turn might obey heaven. I know the weakness of this teaching and that the superiority of Christianity is nowhere more manifest than here, in that it requires of each and every living soul direct responsibility to its Creator. Nevertheless, as far as the doctrine of service—the serving of a cause higher than one's own self, even at the sacrifice of one's individuality; I say the doctrine of service, which is the greatest that Christ preached and is the sacred keynote of his mission—as far as that is concerned, Bushido is based on eternal truth.

My readers will not accuse me of undue prejudice in favor of slavish surrender of volition. I accept in a large measure the view advanced with breadth of learning and defended with profundity of thought by Hegel, that history is the unfolding and realization of freedom. The point I wish to make is that the whole teaching of Bushido was so thoroughly imbued with the spirit of self-sacrifice, that it was required not only of woman but of man. Hence, until the influence of its Precepts is entirely done away with, our society will not realize the view rashly expressed by an American exponent of woman's rights, who exclaimed, "May all the daughters of Japan rise in revolt against ancient customs!" Can such a revolt succeed? Will it improve the female status? Will the rights they gain by such a summary process repay the loss of that sweetness of disposition, that gentleness of manner, which are their present heritage? Was not the loss of domesticity on the part of Roman matrons followed by moral corruption too gross to mention? Can the American reformer assure us that a revolt of our daughters is the true course for their historical development to take? These are grave questions. Changes must and will come without revolts! In the meantime let us see whether the status of the fair sex under the Bushido regimen was really so bad as to justify a revolt.

*'Fulling Cloth at the Jewel River (*Kinuta no Tamagawa*),' by Suzuki Harunobu. This print illustrates two women, probably a mother and daughter, beating cloth under a candle hung on the pillar in an earthen-floored room.*

Act Two, 'The House of Kakogawa Honzo', from the play Chushingura (Treasury of Loyal Retainers), *1774–85. This scene introduces the classic theme of a young betrothed couple torn between their mutual love for each other and the family loyalties that divide them. The samurai is Rikiya, one of Lord Asano's retainers and the son of Kuranosuke, chamberlain and leader of the 47 samurai retainers. His betrothed is Konami, daughter of Honzo, a chief retainer to the shogun.*

We hear much of the outward respect European knights paid to "God and the ladies"—the incongruity of the two terms making Gibbon blush; we are also told by Hallam that the morality of Chivalry was coarse, that gallantry implied illicit love. The effect of Chivalry on the weaker vessel was food for reflection on the part of philosophers, M. Guizot contending that Feudalism and Chivalry wrought wholesome influences, while Mr. Spencer tells us that in a militant society (and what is feudal society if not militant?) the position of woman is necessarily low, improving only as society becomes more industrial. Now is M. Guizot's theory true of Japan, or is Mr. Spencer's? In reply I might aver that both are right. The military class in Japan was restricted to the samurai, comprising nearly 2,000,000 souls. Above them were the military nobles, the *daimio*, and the court nobles, the *kugé*—these higher, sybaritical nobles being fighters only in name. Below them were masses of the common people—mechanics, tradesmen, and peasants—whose life was devoted to arts of peace. Thus what Herbert Spencer gives as the characteristics of a militant type of society may be said to have been exclusively confined to the samurai class, while those of the industrial type were applicable to the classes above and below it. This is well illustrated by the position of woman; for in no class did she experience less freedom than among the samurai. Strange to say, the lower the social class—as, for instance, among small artisans—the more equal was the position of husband and wife. Among the higher nobility, too, the difference in the relations of the sexes was less marked, chiefly because there were few occasions to bring the differences of sex into prominence, the leisurely nobleman having become literally effeminate. Thus Spencer's dictum was fully exemplified in Old Japan. As to Guizot's, those who read his presentation of a feudal community will remember that he had the higher nobility especially under consideration, so that his generalization applies to the *daimio* and the *kugé*.

I shall be guilty of gross injustice to historical truth if my words give one a very low opinion of the status of woman under Bushido. I do not hesitate to state that she was not treated as man's equal; but until we learn to discriminate between difference and inequalities, there will always be misunderstandings upon this subject.

When we think in how few respects men are equal among themselves, *e.g.*, before law courts or voting polls, it seems idle to trouble ourselves with a discussion on the equality of sexes. When, the American Declaration of Independence said that all men were created equal, it had no reference to their mental or physical gifts: it simply repeated what Ulpian long ago announced, that before the law all men are equal. Legal rights were in this case the measure of their equality. Were the law the only scale by which to measure the position of woman in a community, it would be as easy to tell where she stands as to give her avoirdupois in pounds and ounces. But the question is: Is there a correct standard in comparing the relative social position of the sexes? Is it right, is it enough, to compare woman's status to man's as the value of silver is compared with that of gold, and give the ratio numerically? Such a method of calculation excludes from consideration the most important kind of value which a human being possesses; namely, the intrinsic. In view of the manifold variety of requisites for making each sex fulfil its earthly mission, the standard to be adopted in measuring its relative position must be of a composite character; or, to borrow from economic language, it must be a multiple standard. Bushido had a standard of its own and it was binomial. It tried to gauge the value of woman on the battlefield and by the hearth. There she counted for very little; here for all. The treatment accorded her corresponded to this double measurement—as a social-political unit not much, while as wife and mother she received highest respect and deepest affection. Why among so military a nation as the Romans, were their matrons so highly venerated? Was it not because they were *matrona*, mothers? Not as fighters or law-givers, but as their mothers did men bow before them. So with us. While fathers and husbands were absent in field or camp, the government of the household was left entirely in the hands of mothers and wives. The education of the young, even their defence, was entrusted to them. The warlike exercises of women, of which I have spoken, were primarily to enable them intelligently to direct and follow the education of their children.

I have noticed a rather superficial notion prevailing among half-informed foreigners, that because the common Japanese expression for one's wife is "my rustic wife" and the like, she is despised and

'Mother and Son by a Mosquito Net' (c. 1769), by Suzuki Harunobu.

held in little esteem. When it is told that such phrases as "my foolish father," "my swinish son," "my awkward self," etc., are in current use, is not the answer clear enough?

To me it seems that our idea of marital union goes in some ways further than the so-called Christian. "Man and woman shall be one flesh." The individualism of the Anglo-Saxon cannot let go of the idea that husband and wife are two persons—hence when they disagree, their separate *rights* are recognized, and when they agree, they exhaust their vocabulary in all sorts of silly pet-names and nonsensical blandishments. It sounds highly irrational to our ears, when a husband or wife speaks to a third party of his other half—better or worse—as being lovely, bright, kind, and what not. Is it good taste to speak of one's self as "my bright self," "my lovely disposition," and so forth? We think praising one's own wife or one's own husband is praising a part of one's own self, and self-praise is regarded, to say the least, as bad taste among us—and I hope, among Christian nations too! I have diverged at some length because the polite debasement of one's consort was a usage most in vogue among the samurai.

The Teutonic races beginning their tribal life with a superstitious awe of the fair sex (though this is really wearing off in Germany!), and the Americans beginning their social life under the painful consciousness of the numerical insufficiency of women[27] (who, now increasing, are, I am afraid, fast losing the prestige their colonial mothers enjoyed), the respect man pays to woman has in Western civilization become the chief standard of morality. But in the martial ethics of Bushido, the main water-shed dividing the good and the bad was sought elsewhere. It was located along the line of duty which bound man to his own divine soul and then to other souls, in the five relations I have mentioned in the early part of this paper. Of these we have brought to our reader's notice, Loyalty, the relation between one man as vassal and another as lord. Upon the rest, I have only dwelt incidentally as occasion presented itself; because they were not peculiar to Bushido. Being founded on natural affections, they could but be common to all mankind, though in some particulars

[27] I refer to those days when girls were imported from England and given in marriage for so many pounds of tobacco, etc.

they may have been accentuated by conditions which its teachings induced. In this connection, there comes before me the peculiar strength and tenderness of friendship between man and man, which often added to the bond of brotherhood a romantic attachment doubtless intensified by the separation of the sexes in youth—a separation which denied to affection the natural channel open to it in Western chivalry or in the free intercourse of Anglo-Saxon lands. I might fill pages with Japanese versions of the story of Damon and Pythias or Achilles and Patroclos, or tell in Bushido parlance of ties as sympathetic as those which bound David and Jonathan.

It is not surprising, however, that the virtues and teachings unique in the Precepts of Knighthood did not remain circumscribed to the military class. This makes us hasten to the consideration of the influence of Bushido on the nation at large.

CHAPTER 15

武士道の影響

The Influence of Bushido

So far we have brought into view only a few of the more prominent peaks which rise above the range of knightly virtues, in themselves so much more elevated than the general level of our national life. As the sun in its rising first tips the highest peaks with russet hue, and then gradually casts its rays on the valley below, so the ethical system which first enlightened the military order drew in course of time followers from amongst the masses. Democracy raises up a natural prince for its leader, and aristocracy infuses a princely spirit among the people. Virtues are no less contagious than vices. "There needs but one wise man in a company, and all are wise, so rapid is the contagion," says Emerson. No social class or caste can resist the diffusive power of moral influence.

Prate as we may of the triumphant march of Anglo-Saxon liberty, rarely has it received impetus from the masses. Was it not rather the work of the squires and *gentlemen*? Very truly does M. Taine say, "These three syllables, as used across the channel, summarize the history of English society." Democracy may make self-confident retorts to such a statement and fling back the question—"When Adam delved and Eve span, where then was the gentleman?" All the more pity that a gentleman was not present in Eden! The first parents missed him sorely and paid a high price for his absence. Had he been there, not only would the garden have been more tastefully dressed, but they would have learned without painful experience that disobedience to Jehovah was disloyalty and dishonor, treason and rebellion.

Man holding up a magnifying glass to examine the famous samurai swordsman Miyamoto Musashi.

Minamoto Yoshitsune and his retainer, the monk Benkei, putting to flight the ghost of Taira no Tomomori.

What Japan was she owed to the samurai. They were not only the flower of the nation but its root as well. All the gracious gifts of Heaven flowed through them. Though they kept themselves socially aloof from the populace, they set a moral standard for them and guided them by their example. I admit Bushido had its esoteric and exoteric teachings; these were eudemonistic, looking after the welfare and happiness of the commonalty, while those were aretaic, emphasizing the practice of virtues for their own sake.

In the most chivalrous days of Europe, Knights formed numerically but a small fraction of the population, but, as Emerson says: "In English Literature half the drama and all the novels, from Sir Philip Sidney to Sir Walter Scott, paint this figure (gentleman)." Write in place of Sidney and Scott, Chikamatsu and Bakin, and you have in a nutshell the main features of the literary history of Japan.

The innumerable avenues of popular amusement and instruction—the theaters, the story-tellers' booths, the preacher's dais, the musical recitations, the novels—have taken for their chief theme the stories of the samurai. The peasants round the open fire in their huts never tire of repeating the achievements of Yoshitsuné and his faithful retainer Benkei, or of the two brave Soga brothers; the dusky urchins listen with gaping mouths until the last stick burns out and the fire dies in its embers, still leaving their hearts aglow with the tale that is told. The clerks and the shop-boys, after their day's work is over and the *amado*[28] of the store are closed, gather together to relate the story of Nobunaga and Hidéyoshi far into the night, until slumber overtakes their weary eyes and transports them from the drudgery of the counter to the exploits of the field. The very babe just beginning to toddle is taught to lisp the adventures of Momotaro, the daring conqueror of ogre-land. Even girls are so imbued with the love of knightly deeds and virtues that, like Desdemona, they would seriously incline to devour with greedy ear the romance of the samurai.

The samurai grew to be the *beau ideal* of the whole race. "As among flowers the cherry is queen, so among men the samurai is lord," so sang the populace. Debarred from commercial pursuits, the

[28] Outside shutters.

military class itself did not aid commerce; but there was no channel of human activity, no avenue of thought, which did not receive in some measure an impetus from Bushido. Intellectual and moral Japan was directly or indirectly the work of Knighthood.

Mr. Mallock, in his exceedingly suggestive book, "Aristocracy and Evolution," has eloquently told us that "social evolution, in so far as it is other than biological, may be defined as the unintended result of the intentions of great men;" further, that historical progress is produced by a struggle "not among the community generally, to live, but a struggle amongst a small section of the community to lead, to direct, to employ, the majority in the best way." Whatever may be said about the soundness of his argument, these statements are amply verified in the part played by *bushi* in the social progress, as far as it went, of our Empire.

How the spirit of Bushido permeated all social classes is also shown in the development of a certain order of men, known as *otoko-daté*, the natural leaders of democracy. Staunch fellows were they, every inch of them strong with the strength of massive manhood. At once the spokesmen and the guardians of popular rights, they had each a following of hundreds and thousands of souls who proffered in the same fashion that samurai did to *daimio*, the willing service of "limb and life, of body, chattels and earthly honor." Backed by a vast multitude of rash and impetuous working-men, those born "bosses" formed a formidable check to the rampancy of the two-sworded order.

In manifold ways has Bushido filtered down from the social class where it originated, and acted as leaven among the masses, furnishing a moral standard for the whole people. The Precepts of Knighthood, begun at first as the glory of the elite, became in time an aspiration and inspiration to the nation at large; and though the populace could not attain the moral height of those loftier souls, yet *Yamato Damashii*, the Soul of Japan, ultimately came to express the *Volksgeist* of the Island Realm. If religion is no more than "Morality touched by emotion," as Matthew Arnold defines it, few ethical systems are better entitled to the rank of religion than Bushido. Motoori has put the mute utterance of the nation into words when he sings:

The assault by Akechi Mitsuhide and the death of the great Oda Nobunaga at the Honnō-ji temple in Kyoto on 21 June 1582.

"Isles of blest Japan!
Should your Yamato spirit
Strangers seek to scan,
Say—scenting morn's sun-lit air,
Blows the cherry wild and fair!"

Yes, the *sakura*[29] has for ages been the favorite of our people and the emblem of our character. Mark particularly the terms of definition which the poet uses, the words the *wild cherry flower scenting the morning sun.*

The Yamato spirit is not a tame, tender plant, but a wild—in the sense of natural—growth; it is indigenous to the soil; its accidental qualities it may share with the flowers of other lands, but in its essence it remains the original, spontaneous outgrowth of our clime. But its nativity is not its sole claim to our affection. The refinement and grace of its beauty appeal to *our* aesthetic sense as no other flower can. We cannot share the admiration of the Europeans for their roses, which lack the simplicity of our flower. Then, too, the thorns that are hidden beneath the sweetness of the rose, the tenacity with which she clings to life, as though loth or afraid to die rather than drop untimely, preferring to rot on her stem; her showy colors and heavy odors—all these are traits so unlike our flower, which carries no dagger or poison under its beauty, which is ever ready to depart life at the call of nature, whose colors are never gorgeous, and whose light fragrance never palls. Beauty of color and of form is limited in its showing; it is a fixed quality of existence, whereas fragrance is volatile, ethereal as the breathing of life. So in all religious ceremonies frankincense and myrrh play a prominent part. There is something spirituelle in redolence. When the delicious perfume of the *sakura* quickens the morning air, as the sun in its course rises to illumine first the isles of the Far East, few sensations are more serenely exhilarating than to inhale, as it were, the very breath of beauteous day.

When the Creator himself is pictured as making new resolutions in his heart upon smelling a sweet savor (Genesis VIII, 21), is it any wonder that the sweet-smelling season of the cherry blossom should

[29] *Cerasus pseudo-cerasus,* Lindley.

call forth the whole nation from their little habitations? Blame them not, if for a time their limbs forget their toil and moil and their hearts their pangs and sorrows. Their brief pleasure ended, they return to their daily tasks with new strength and new resolutions. Thus in ways more than one is the sakura the flower of the nation.

Is, then, this flower, so sweet and evanescent, blown whithersoever the wind listeth, and, shedding a puff of perfume, ready to vanish forever, is this flower the type of the Yamato spirit? Is the Soul of Japan so frailly mortal?

CHAPTER 16

武士道未だ生きてるのか

Is Bushido Still Alive?

Or has Western civilization, in its march through the land, already wiped out every trace of its ancient discipline?

It were a sad thing if a nation's soul could die so fast. That were a poor soul that could succumb so easily to extraneous influences. The aggregate of psychological elements which constitute a national character, is as tenacious as the "irreducible elements of species, of the fins of fish, of the beak of the bird, of the tooth of the carnivorous animal." In his recent book, full of shallow asseverations and brilliant generalizations, M. LeBon[30] says, "The discoveries due to the intelligence are the common patrimony of humanity; qualities or defects of character constitute the exclusive patrimony of each people: they are the firm rock which the waters must wash day by day for centuries, before they can wear away even its external asperities." These are strong words and would be highly worth pondering over, provided there were qualities and defects of character which *constitute the exclusive patrimony* of each people. Schematizing theories of this sort had been advanced long before LeBon began to write his book, and they were exploded long ago by Theodor Waitz and Hugh Murray. In studying the various virtues instilled by Bushido, we have drawn upon European sources for comparison and illustrations, and we have seen that no one quality of character was its *exclusive* patrimony. It is true the aggregate of moral qualities presents a quite unique aspect. It is this aggregate which Emerson names a "compound result into which every great force enters as an ingredient." But, instead of making it, as LeBon does, an exclusive patrimony of a race or people, the Concord philosopher calls it "an element which unites the most forcible persons of every country; makes

[30] *The Psychology of Peoples*, p. 33.

Dutch and German businessmen drafting a contract in a Yokohama mercantile house, 1861.

them intelligible and agreeable to each other; and is somewhat so precise that it is at once felt if an individual lack the Masonic sign."

The character which Bushido stamped on our nation and on the samurai in particular, cannot be said to form "an irreducible element of species," but nevertheless as to the vitality which it retains there is no doubt. Were Bushido a mere physical force, the momentum it has gained in the last seven hundred years could not stop so abruptly. Were it transmitted only by heredity, its influence must be immensely widespread. Just think, as M. Cheysson, a French economist, has calculated, that supposing there be three generations in a century, "each of us would have in his veins the blood of at least twenty millions of the people living in the year 1000 A.D." The merest peasant that grubs the soil, "bowed by the weight of centuries," has in his veins the blood of ages, and is thus a brother to us as much as "to the ox."

An unconscious and irresistible power, Bushido has been moving the nation and individuals. It was an honest confession of the race when Yoshida Shoin, one of the most brilliant pioneers of Modern Japan, wrote on the eve of his execution the following stanza:

"Full well I knew this course must end in death;
It was Yamato spirit urged me on
To dare whate'er betide."

Unformulated, Bushido was and still is the animating spirit, the motor force of our country.

Mr. Ransome says that "there are three distinct Japans in existence side by side today—the old, which has not wholly died out; the new, hardly yet born except in spirit; and the transition, passing now through its most critical throes." While this is very true in most respects, and particularly as regards tangible and concrete institutions, the statement, as applied to fundamental ethical notions, requires some modification; for Bushido, the maker and product of Old Japan, is still the guiding principle of the transition and will prove the formative force of the new era.

The great statesmen who steered the ship of our state through

Bugler Shirakami, heavily wounded and facing death at the ford of Ancheng, continues to sound the advance, 1894.

the hurricane of the Restoration and the whirlpool of national rejuvenation, were men who knew no other moral teaching than the Precepts of Knighthood. Some writers[31] have lately tried to prove that the Christian missionaries contributed an appreciable quota to the making of New Japan. I would fain render honor to whom honor is due: but this honor can hardly be accorded to the good missionaries. More fitting it will be to their profession to stick to the scriptural injunction of preferring one another in honor, than to advance a claim in which they have no proofs to back them. For myself, I believe that Christian missionaries are doing great things for Japan—in the domain of education, and especially of moral education—only, the mysterious though not the less certain working of the Spirit is still hidden in divine secrecy. Whatever they do is still of indirect effect. No, as yet Christian missions have effected but little visible in moulding the character of New Japan. No, it was Bushido, pure and simple, that urged us on for weal or woe. Open the biographies of the makers of Modern Japan—of Sakuma, of Saigo, of Okubo, of Kido, not to mention the reminiscences of living men such as Ito, Okuma, Itagaki, etc.—and you will find that it was under the impetus of samuraihood that they thought and wrought. When Mr. Henry Norman declared, after his study and observation of the Far East,[32] that only the respect in which Japan differed from other oriental despotisms lay in "the ruling influence among her people of the strictest, loftiest, and the most punctilious codes of honor that man has ever devised," he touched the main spring which has made new Japan what she is and which will make her what she is destined to be.

The transformation of Japan is a fact patent to the whole world. In a work of such magnitude various motives naturally entered; but if one were to name the principal, one would not hesitate to name Bushido. When we opened the whole country to foreign trade, when we introduced the latest improvements in every department of life, when we began to study Western politics and sciences, our guiding motive was not the development of our physical resources and the increase of wealth; much less was it a blind imitation of Western customs. A close observer of oriental institutions and peoples has written: "We are told every day how Europe has influenced Japan,

[31] Speer; *Missions and Politics in Asia*, Lecture IV, pp. 189–190; Dennis: *Christian Missions and Social Progress*, Vol. I, p. 32, Vol. II, p. 70, etc.

[32] *The Far East*, p. 375.

A young samurai is concerned about Japan's future during the Ansei Purge (1858–60). Tokugawa bakuhu keijizufu, *published in Meiji 26 (1893).*

and forget that the change in those islands was entirely self-generated, that Europeans did not teach Japan, but that Japan of herself chose to learn from Europe methods of organization, civil and military, which have so far proved successful. She imported European mechanical science, as the Turks years before imported European artillery. That is not exactly influence," continues Mr. Townsend, "unless, indeed, England is influenced by purchasing tea of China. Where is the European apostle," asks our author, "or philosopher or statesman or agitator who has re-made Japan?"[33] Mr. Townsend has well perceived that the spring of action which brought about the changes in Japan lay entirely within our own selves; and if he had only probed into our psychology, his keen powers of observation would easily have convinced him that that spring was no other than Bushido. The sense of honor which cannot bear being looked down upon as an inferior power—that was the strongest of motives. Pecuniary or industrial considerations were awakened later in the process of transformation.

The influence of Bushido is still so palpable that he who runs may read. A glimpse into Japanese life will make it manifest. Read Hearn, the most eloquent and truthful interpreter of the Japanese mind, and you see the working of that mind to be an example of the working of Bushido. The universal politeness of the people, which is the legacy of knightly ways, is too well known to be repeated anew. The physical endurance, fortitude and bravery that "the little Jap" possesses, were sufficiently proved in the China-Japanese war.[34] "Is there any nation more loyal and patriotic?" is a question asked by many; and for the proud answer, "There is not," we must thank the Precepts of Knighthood.

On the other hand, it is fair to recognize that for the very faults and defects of our character, Bushido is largely responsible. Our lack of abstruse philosophy—while some of our young men have already gained international reputation in scientific researches, not one has achieved anything in philosophical lines—is traceable to the neglect of metaphysical training under Bushido's regimen of education. Our sense of honor is responsible for our exaggerated sensitiveness

[33] Meredith Townsend, *Asia and Europe*, N.Y., 1900, p. 28.

[34] Among other works on the subject, read Eastlake and Yamada on *Heroic Japan*, and Diosy on *The New Far East*.

and touchiness; and if there is the conceit in us with which some foreigners charge us, that, too, is a pathological outcome of honor.

Have you seen in your tour of Japan many a young man with unkempt hair, dressed in shabbiest garb, carrying in his hand a large cane or a book, stalking about the streets with an air of utter indifference to mundane things? He is the *shosei* (student), to whom the earth is too small and the Heavens are not high enough. He has his own theories of the universe and of life. He dwells in castles of air and feeds on ethereal words of wisdom. In his eyes beams the fire of ambition; his mind is athirst for knowledge. Penury is only a stimulus to drive him onward; worldly goods are in his sight shackles to his character. He is the repository of Loyalty and Patriotism. He is the self-imposed guardian of national honor. With all his virtues and his faults, he is the last fragment of Bushido.

Deep-rooted and powerful as is still the effect of Bushido, I have said that it is an unconscious and mute influence. The heart of the people responds, without knowing the reason why, to any appeal made to what it has inherited, and hence the same moral idea expressed in a newly translated term and in an old Bushido term, has a vastly different degree of efficacy. A backsliding Christian, whom no pastoral persuasion could help from downward tendency, was reverted from his course by an appeal made to his loyalty, the fidelity he once swore to his Master. The word "Loyalty" revived all the noble sentiments that were permitted to grow lukewarm. A band of unruly youths engaged in a long continued "students' strike" in a college, on account of their dissatisfaction with a certain teacher, disbanded at two simple questions put by the Director—"Is your professor a blameless character? If so, you ought to respect him and keep him in the school. Is he weak? If so, it is not manly to push a falling man." The scientific incapacity of the professor, which was the beginning of the trouble, dwindled into insignificance in comparison with the moral issues hinted at. By arousing the sentiments nurtured by Bushido, moral renovation of great magnitude can be accomplished.

One cause of the failure of mission work is that most of the missionaries are grossly ignorant of our history—"What do we care for heathen records?" some say—and consequently estrange their

Two Jesuit priests, early seventeenth century. Detail from a folding screen.

religion from the habits of thought we and our forefathers have been accustomed to for centuries past. Mocking a nation's history! As though the career of any people—even of the lowest African savages possessing no record—were not a page in the general history of mankind, written by the hand of God Himself. The very lost races are a palimpsest to be deciphered by a seeing eye. To a philosophic and pious mind, the races themselves are marks of Divine chirography clearly traced in black and white as on their skin; and if this simile holds good, the yellow race forms a precious page inscribed in hieroglyphics of gold! Ignoring the past career of a people, missionaries claim that Christianity is a new religion, whereas, to my mind, it is an "old, old story," which, if presented in intelligible words—that is to say, if expressed in the vocabulary familiar in the moral development of a people—will find easy lodgment in their hearts, irrespective of race or nationality. Christianity in its American or English form—with more of Anglo-Saxon freaks and fancies than grace and purity of its founder—is a poor scion to graft on Bushido stock. Should the propagator of the new faith uproot the entire stock, root and branches, and plant the seeds of the Gospel on the ravaged soil? Such a heroic process may be possible—in Hawaii, where, it is alleged, the church militant had complete success in amassing spoils of wealth itself, and in annihilating the aboriginal race: such a process is most decidedly impossible in Japan—nay, it is a process which Jesus himself would never have employed in founding his kingdom on earth. It behooves us to take more to heart the following words of a saintly man, devout Christian and profound scholar: "Men have divided the world into heathen and Christian, without considering how much good may have been hidden in the one, or how much evil may have been mingled with the other. They have compared the best part of themselves with the worst of their neighbors, the ideal of Christianity with the corruption of Greece or the East. They have not aimed at impartiality, but have been contented to accumulate all that could be said in praise of their own, and in dispraise of other forms of religion."[35]

But, whatever may be the error committed by individuals, there is little doubt that the fundamental principle of the religion they profess is a power which we must take into account in reckoning the future of Bushido.

[35] Jowett, *Sermons on Faith and Doctrine*, II.

CHAPTER 17

武士道が遺したもの

The Future of Bushido

Bushido's days seem to be already numbered. Ominous signs are in the air that betoken its future. Not only signs, but redoubtable forces are at work to threaten it.

Few historical comparisons can be more judiciously made than between the Chivalry of Europe and the Bushido of Japan, and, if history repeats itself, it certainly will do with the fate of the latter what it did with that of the former. The particular and local causes for the decay of Chivalry which St. Palaye gives, have, of course, little application to Japanese conditions; but the larger and more general causes that helped to undermine Knighthood and Chivalry in and after the Middle Ages are as surely working for the decline of Bushido.

One remarkable difference between the experience of Europe and of Japan is, that, whereas in Europe when Chivalry was weaned from Feudalism and was adopted by the Church, it obtained a fresh lease of life, in Japan no religion was large enough to nourish it; hence, when the mother institution, Feudalism, was gone, Bushido, left an orphan, had to shift for itself. The present elaborate military organization might take it under its patronage, but we know that modern warfare can afford little room for its continuous growth. Shintoism, which fostered it in its infancy, is itself superannuated. The hoary sages of ancient China are being supplanted by the intellectual parvenu of the type of Bentham and Mill. Moral theories of a comfortable kind, flattering to the Chauvinistic tendencies of the time, and therefore thought well-adapted to the need of this day, have been invented and propounded; but as yet we hear only their shrill voices echoing through the columns of yellow journalism.

An American merchant strolling in Yokohama.

Principalities and powers are arrayed against the Precepts of Knighthood. Already, as Veblen says, "the decay of the ceremonial code—or, as it is otherwise called, the vulgarization of life—among the industrial classes proper, has become one of the chief enormities of latter-day civilization in the eyes of all persons of delicate sensibilities." The irresistible tide of triumphant democracy, which can tolerate no form or shape of trust—and Bushido was a trust organized by those who monopolized reserve capital of intellect and culture, fixing the grades and value of moral qualities—is alone powerful enough to engulf the remnant of Bushido. The present societary forces are antagonistic to petty class spirit, and Chivalry is, as Freeman severely criticizes, a class spirit. Modern society, if it pretends to any unity, cannot admit "purely personal obligations devised in the interests of an exclusive class."[36] Add to this the progress of popular instruction, of industrial arts and habits, of wealth and city-life, then we can easily see that neither the keenest cuts of samurai's sword nor the sharpest shafts shot from Bushido's boldest bows can aught avail. The state built upon the rock of Honor and fortified by the same—shall we call it the *Ehrenstaat* or, after the manner of Carlyle, the Heroarchy—is fast falling into the hands of quibbling lawyers and gibbering politicians armed with logic-chopping engines of war. The words which a great thinker used in speaking of Theresa and Antigone may aptly be repeated of the samurai, that "the medium in which their ardent deeds took shape is forever gone."

Alas for knightly virtues! alas for samurai pride! Morality ushered into the world with the sound of bugles and drums, is destined to fade away as "the captains and the kings depart."

If history can teach us anything, the state built on martial virtues—be it a city like Sparta or an Empire like Rome—can never make on earth a "continuing city." Universal and natural as is the fighting instinct in man, fruitful as it has proved to be of noble sentiments and manly virtues, it does not comprehend the whole man. Beneath the instinct to fight there lurks a diviner instinct to love. We have seen that Shintoism, Mencius and Wan Yang Ming, have all clearly taught it; but Bushido and all other militant schools

[36] *Norman Conquest*, Vol. V, p. 482.

A close-up of a traditional samurai armed with a wakizashi, *or short sword. From a late nineteenth century woodcut by Utagawa Kunikazu.*

This samurai is armed with two swords—the longer katana *and shorter* wakizashi*—as well as a bow, or* yumi*. The* yumi *was traditionally over 6.5 feet (2m) in length, providing the archer with accuracy at long range.*

of ethics, engrossed, doubtless, with questions of immediate practical need, too often forgot duly to emphasize this fact. Life has grown larger in these latter times. Callings nobler and broader than a warrior's claim our attention today. With an enlarged view of life, with the growth of democracy, with better knowledge of other peoples and nations, the Confucian idea of Benevolence (dare I also add the Buddhist idea of Pity?) will expand into the Christian conception of Love. Men have become more than subjects, having grown to the estate of citizens: nay, they are more than citizens, being men.

Though war clouds hang heavy upon our horizon, we will believe that the wings of the angel of peace can disperse them. The history of the world confirms the prophecy that "the meek shall inherit the earth." A nation that sells its birthright of peace, and backslides from the front rank of Industrialism into the file of Filibusterism, makes a poor bargain indeed!

When the conditions of society are so changed that they have become not only adverse but hostile to Bushido, it is time for it to prepare for an honorable burial. It is just as difficult to point out when chivalry dies, as to determine the exact time of its inception. Dr. Miller says that Chivalry was formally abolished in the year 1559, when Henry II of France was slain in a tournament. With us, the edict formally abolishing Feudalism in 1870 was the signal to toll the knell of Bushido. The edict, issued two years later, prohibiting the wearing of swords, rang out the old, "the unbought grace of life, the cheap defence of nations, the nurse of manly sentiment and heroic enterprise," it rang in the new age of "sophisters, economists, and calculators."

It has been said that Japan won her late war with China by means of Murata guns and Krupp cannon; it has been said the victory was the work of a modern school system; but these are less than half-truths. Does ever a piano, be it of the choicest workmanship of Ehrbar or Steinway, burst forth into the Rhapsodies of Liszt or the Sonatas of Beethoven, without a master's hand? Or, if guns win battles, why did not Louis Napoleon beat the Prussians with his *Mitrailleuse,* or the Spaniards with their Mausers the Filipinos, whose arms were no better than the

old-fashioned Remingtons? Needless to repeat what has grown a trite saying that it is the spirit that quickeneth, without which the best of implements profiteth but little. The most improved guns and cannon do not shoot of their own accord; the most modern educational system does not make a coward a hero. No! What won the battles on the Yalu, in Corea and Manchuria, was the ghosts of our fathers, guiding our hands and beating in our hearts. They are not dead, those ghosts, the spirits of our warlike ancestors. To those who have eyes to see, they are clearly visible. Scratch a Japanese of the most advanced ideas, and he will show a samurai. The great inheritance of honor, of valor and of all martial virtues is, as Professor Cramb very fitly expresses it, "but ours on trust, the fief inalienable of the dead and of the generation to come," and the summons of the present is to guard this heritage, nor to bate one jot of the ancient spirit; the summons of the future will be so to widen its scope as to apply it in all walks and relations of life.

It has been predicted—and predictions have been corroborated by the events of the last half century—that the moral system of Feudal Japan, like its castles and its armories, will crumble into dust, and new ethics rise phoenix-like to lead New Japan in her path of progress. Desirable and probable as the fulfilment of such a prophecy is, we must not forget that a phoenix rises only from its own ashes, and that it is not a bird of passage, neither does it fly on pinions borrowed from other birds. "The Kingdom of God is within you." It does not come rolling down the mountains, however lofty; it does not come sailing across the seas, however broad. "God has granted," says the Koran, "to every people a prophet in its own tongue." The seeds of the Kingdom, as vouched for and apprehended by the Japanese mind, blossomed in Bushido. Now its days are closing—sad to say, before its full fruition—and we turn in every direction for other sources of sweetness and light, of strength and comfort, but among them there is as yet nothing found to take its place. The profit and loss philosophy of Utilitarians and Materialists finds favor among logic-choppers with half a soul. The only other ethical system which is powerful enough to cope with Utilitarianism and Materialism is Christianity, in comparison with which Bushido, it must be confessed, is like "a dimly burning wick" which the Messiah was proclaimed not to quench but to fan into a flame. Like His Hebrew precursors, the prophets—notably Isaiah, Jeremiah, Amos and Habakkuk—Bushido

'Moon over Shinobugaoka.' A young samurai warrior, Gyokuensai, is startled by the wind blowing blossom petals.

'Weeping Cherry', by Utagawa Hiroshige.

laid particular stress on the moral conduct of rulers and public men and of nations, whereas the Ethics of Christ, which deal almost solely with individuals and His personal followers, will find more and more practical application as individualism, in its capacity of a moral factor, grows in potency. The domineering, self-assertive, so-called master-morality of Nietzsche, itself akin in some respects to Bushido, is, if I am not greatly mistaken, a passing phase or temporary reaction against what he terms, by morbid distortion, the humble, self-denying slave-morality of the Nazarene.

Christianity and Materialism (including Utilitarianism)—or will the future reduce them to still more archaic forms of Hebraism and Hellenism?—will divide the world between them. Lesser systems of morals will ally themselves on either side for their preservation. On which side will Bushido enlist? Having no set dogma or formula to defend, it can afford to disappear as an entity; like the cherry blossom, it is willing to die at the first gust of the morning breeze. But a total extinction will never be its lot. Who can say that stoicism is dead? It is dead as a system; but it is alive as a virtue: its energy and vitality are still felt through many channels of life—in the philosophy of Western nations, in the jurisprudence of all the civilized world. Nay, wherever man struggles to raise himself above himself, wherever his spirit masters his flesh by his own exertions, there we see the immortal discipline of Zeno at work.

Bushido as an independent code of ethics may vanish, but its power will not perish from the earth; its schools of martial prowess or civic honor may be demolished, but its light and its glory will long survive their ruins. Like its symbolic flower, after it is blown to the four winds, it will still bless mankind with the perfume with which it will enrich life. Ages after, when its customaries shall have been buried and its very name forgotten, its odors will come floating in the air as from a far-off unseen hill, "the wayside gaze beyond"—then in the beautiful language of the Quaker poet,

> "The traveler owns the grateful sense
> Of sweetness near he knows not whence,
> And, pausing, takes with forehead bare
> The benediction of the air."

Index